Integrating Outcome Research Into Counseling Practice and Training

Thomas L. Sexton
Susan C. Whiston
University of Nevada, Las Vegas

Jeanne C. Bleuer
Garry R. Walz
University of North Carolina-Greensboro

INTEGRATING OUTCOME RESEARCH INTO COUNSELING PRACTICE AND TRAINING

10 9 8 7 6 5 4 3 2

American Counseling Association
5999 Stevenson Avenue
Alexandria, VA 22304

Director of Acquisitions
Carolyn Baker

Director of Publishing Systems
Michael Comlish

Cover design by Jennifer Sterling, Spot Color

Library of Congress Cataloging-in-Publication Data

Integrating outcome research into counseling practice and training /
    Thomas L. Sexton . . . [et al.].
        p.   cm.
    Includes bibliographical references and index.
      ISBN 1-55620-171-0 (alk. paper)
      1. Counseling.   2. Counselors—Training of.   I. Sexton, Thomas
L., 1953–   .
    BF637.C6I6152   1997
    361'.06—DC21

Table of Contents

About the Authors

THOMAS L. SEXTON is an associate professor in the Department of Counseling at the University of Nevada, Las Vegas. He is a graduate of Florida State University with a Ph.D. in counseling psychology. He is a licensed psychologist with interests in the counseling process. His research focus has been the systematic study of counseling outcome and process research and its application to counseling practice. He is on the Editorial Board of *Counselor Education and Supervision* and is the author of numerous articles in the area of counseling effectiveness.

SUSAN C. WHISTON is an associate professor in the Department of Educational Psychology at the University of Nevada, Las Vegas. She received her Ph.D. at the University of Wyoming. She is interested in the effectiveness of both career and school counseling interventions and has published extensively in these areas. She is associate editor of the *Journal of Counseling and Development*.

JEANNE C. BLEUER is Associate Director of the ERIC Clearinghouse on Counseling and Student Services and a Senior Research Scientist at the University of North Carolina at Greensboro.

GARRY R. WALZ is Director of the ERIC Clearinghouse on Counseling and Student Services and a Senior Research Scientist at the University of North Carolina at Greensboro. He is a former president of both the American Counseling Association and the Association of Counselor Education and Supervision. He is a frequent writer on topics relating to career, information utilization, and media and technology. He is also Professor Emeritus, University of Michigan.

Preface

The systematic study of counseling occupies a curious position within the counseling profession. Although there is a substantial and growing body of research-based knowledge that is readily applicable, practitioners continue to perceive research as irrelevant, difficult to understand, and impossible to incorporate into daily practice. Consequently, experience, theory, and clinical intuition have come to be the clinical standard—the basis on which most clinical decisions are made and the curricular foundation of many counselor education programs. Through our varied experiences as practitioners, researchers, and educators, we have become skeptical of this standard as the sole basis of clinical decision making. We think that the gap between research and practice is a serious problem that is making it difficult for us to develop and deliver the best possible counseling services. We are of the mind that the key factor in therapeutic behavior change is the way in which broad based and systematic knowledge can be skillfully applied by professional clinicians. That goal can be realized only if research and practice are systematically linked.

The findings of the project reported in this book is the collaboration of two different research groups who had been pursuing the same goals in different ways and through different forums. One team was made up of the senior researchers at ERIC/CASS (Bleuer & Walz). For the ERIC Clearinghouse on Counseling and Student Services (ERIC/CASS), tracking counseling practitioner and researcher and scholar interests is an ongoing major task. In the early 1990s, the tracking and scanning of the questions and documents being received revealed a large increase in the interest expressed by both counseling professionals and the general public in the effectiveness of counseling. This interest paralleled a burgeoning study of the efficacy of various self- and counselor or therapist-initiated interventions targeting improved client behavior. Professional educators and

public reform groups were concurrently calling for renewed attention to educational outcomes and the need to establish educational
goals that would make American education more accountable. The
underlying message was clear: If an educational practice doesn't
work, fix it or eliminate it! Policy studies and the zealous efforts of
local and state groups to improve what students gained from their
schooling were clearly being heard and having an effect.

It was in this national atmosphere of challenge and change that
ERIC/CASS presented an American Counseling Association (ACA)
program at the national convention on "Counselor Efficacy: Assessing and Using Counseling Outcome Research." The enthusiastic
response to the program encouraged us to develop a monograph of
the same title with contributions by the program presenters—Jeanne
Bleuer, Jon Carlson, Rich Feller, Robert Gibson, Cynthia Johnson,
Nancy Perry, Thomas Sexton, and Garry Walz. The response to the
monograph was highly informative and has significantly affected our
subsequent work.

During this same period, the other group (Sexton & Whiston)
were conducting a series of systematic reviews of the outcome
research in various areas of counseling practice. Their work was published in numerous journal articles and presented at national and
regional meetings. Each article and presentation was aimed at systematically distilling the practical implications that might be gained
from applying counseling outcome research to clinical practice.

Along our different paths each of us encountered similar reactions to this work. Typically one group of counselors and counselor
educators was passionately supportive and collectively greeted its
publication with barely contained glee. The comment of one counselor educator clearly expressed the thinking of this group: "Thank
God, we are at last attending to the consequences of counseling and
using it to design our counseling courses and interventions." Our
pleasure at this expression, however, was strongly tempered by a
larger and more pervasive response best described as a large professional yawn!

To many, a concern for counseling and counselor efficacy was the
realm of the researcher, a suitable topic for number crunchers, but
hardly real for educators and practitioners. As best we could understand this perspective, the practice of counseling provided its own
validation and efficacy insights. This "if you do you know" point of

view, we believe, is a strong component of many, if not most, counselor belief systems. To those who wittingly or unwittingly profess this perspective, counseling outcomes research is interesting, but not essential to determining counseling priorities. As others have also noted, research results that are at variance with personal beliefs (frequently cherished and of long duration) have minimal effect on changing counselor planning and practice.

We were, therefore, delighted when the Counseling and Human Development Foundation (CHDF) issued a "Request for Proposals for a Counseling Outcomes Research Literature Review." It offered the opportunity to undertake the comprehensive and intensive collection and review of the counseling outcomes research literature that we felt was highly needed, but required financial resources well beyond those of ERIC/CASS. It also gave us the chance to collaborate and bring together the best of what each research group had been thinking on the role of outcome research in counseling practice.

One of the major objectives of the grant we received from the Counseling and Human Development Foundation of the ACA was to study the extent and applicability of outcome research to counseling practice. Our plan was to develop a systematic outcome research database in the various areas in which counselors practice—mental health, career, and school counseling. We hoped that once established, this database of the available clinical studies and systematic reviews would reveal both a picture of counseling effectiveness and the components that contribute to positive outcomes. Our focus in the project was to look, through the eyes of outcome research, for those factors that directly impact the success or failure of the counseling enterprise. The purpose of this book is to present our findings. Our hope is that this synthesis can serve as a useful beginning in the reintegration of research into counseling practice and clinical decision making.

The work presented here is based on a series of assumptions. First, we see counseling as a common process shared by diverse practitioners, using varied theoretical perspectives, and practiced in diverse settings. Thus, our goal is to present what we know about counseling as a process, irrespective of its theoretical and professional alliances. You will see that we have decided to treat research on counseling and psychotherapy as one and the same. There may be important philosophical differences between the two, but we think it is currently more useful to focus on the broad knowledge base that addresses common behavior-change principles. Within the general domain, we do believe that there is specific knowledge about certain focal areas—mental health, career, and school counseling—that is significant and important. Second, we assume that practice should be informed by systematic research. Given the complexity of outcome research, we think it should be the reliable and valid trends, rather than results of any single study, that influences practice and education. Consequently, conclusions we present here are based on stable trends, across many types of studies, and with varied settings and clients.

Third, we have come to believe that many of the reasons for the research-practice gap are due to a lack of knowledge and awareness rather than because of any justifiable division between these two activities. A unified goal of effective service to clients cannot be achieved until practitioner and researchers forge a closer relationship. In fact, we think research and practice are really only different sides of the same coin—both necessary and neither one alone sufficient. Finally, we believe that the integration of research into practice is imminent. The world of mental health is increasingly being judged based on accountability and research evidence. Even if professional counselors do not take up this call to arms, other professions will. For professional counselors to be credible providers of services and for counselor educators to train new professionals who can successfully compete in this world, we must put the best of our systematic research knowledge at the center of clinical decision making.

Integrating Outcome Research into Counseling Practice and Training is aimed at a wide audience. We think it will be useful to counseling practitioners and educators seeking to include research based information in their work. In addition, students will find the book an easy way to understand the complexities of counseling research. Furthermore, we think it can bring alive the seemingly irrelevant methods of research in a counseling practice setting. We also think the book has applications beyond professional counselors. Social workers and psychologists work within the same counseling process addressed here.

Section I forms the foundation of the book. Chapter 1 is an analysis of the major criticisms of outcome research that hinder its integration into practice. From our perspective these issues need not stand in the way of integration. Chapter 2 is a brief overview of the unique nature of counseling outcome research—its guiding questions, its common methods, its strengths, and weaknesses. Armed with this knowledge, the practitioner can appropriately use the available research findings in clinical practice. For researchers, these chapters provide a perspective on the necessary ingredients for relevant clinical outcome research.

The four chapters in Section II focus on the application of current research-based knowledge to the practice of counseling. We make conclusions and recommendations that are representative of what we identify to be stable trends in the body of outcome research. Our review is organized around an atheoretical process-model. Chapter 3 ("The Effectiveness of Counseling") focuses on the outcomes of counseling. In addition, we address some of the major practical questions regarding counseling: How long does it take?, How long does it last?, Which theories are effective? Chapter 4 focuses on mental health counseling, in which individual counseling is the traditional modality. Many of these findings apply to the broad process of behavior change, across settings and focal areas. In particular, we investigate client–counselor factors, the therapeutic contract, the counseling relationship, as well as the specific techniques that positively contribute to successful counseling. Chapter 5 is a review of the unique research-based trends in career counseling. Chapter 6 is an analysis of the effective components, from a research perspective, of working with children in both therapeutic counseling techniques and school guidance activities.

The final section of the book (Section III) addresses the integration of research into practice. We think that integration will occur only if research is understood, applied, and developed in cooperation with practicing professional counselors. A major hurdle in this task is the great range and diversity of research publications. Chapter 7 focuses on practical techniques that practitioners and researchers alike can gather and use now and in the future. The quintessential question regarding counseling outcome research is not how much has been generated or how good it is (all important!), but how much it is used. The sources and ways people access information, as well as what they believe to be appropriate uses for that information, will strongly affect the extent to which counseling outcome research is used. The goals of the final chapter (Chapter 8) are twofold. First, we present a pragmatic model of the systematic relationship between activities of counseling research and practice, and second, we present a model of action research to help make research a regular part of daily counseling practice.

Important research is frequently undertaken because of the commitment of "gatekeepers" to see that it gets done. Such is very much the case in this research. In their terms as chairs of the Counseling and Human Development Foundation, Mike Robinson and Gloria Smith provided continuing support and interest as we struggled with the vexing problems of acquiring and making sense out of a huge body of information. They and the committees they chaired deserve great credit for recognizing the importance of the topic and seeing us through its completion, despite many frustrating delays. Subsequent chairs, Jane Myers and Don Locke, were also supportive.

Crucial to the substance of this project was the stipulation in the grant that the results be published. The affirmative reaction and positive response to this manuscript made it possible for us to meet the last and important condition of the grant. Special thanks go to Carolyn Baker for her early and continuing interest in the project and her astute shepherding of it through many challenges. We also wish to thank our graduate students, Fran Cannard, Nancy Ostrum, and Lisa Schenk, who spent endless hours tracking down and acquiring the many documents that were reviewed in the project, editing, and helping to develop and manage a huge computer database of outcome studies. Finally, we thank those colleagues who have supported our point of view in the years in which we felt like lone voices in the wind.

As is true of many things in life, a researcher's work is never done. Typically, good research raises as many questions as it answers. We hope that both outcomes—answers and questions—will be useful to you, the reader. This volume is a beginning, not an ending. Future writing will expand the answers provided and raise significant new questions.

The Nature of Counseling Outcome Research

CHAPTER 1

The Impact of Outcome Research in Clinical Decision Making

Across the country we are witnessing tremendous growth in the need for and cost of counseling related services. Consider some examples: About one in five adults suffers from a diagnosable mental disorder ranging from schizophrenia, to depression, to substance abuse (Rice, Kelman, Miller, & Dunmeyer, 1990); in addition, almost 12% of children under 18 experience serious emotional difficulties. Increasing numbers of people are seeking psychological help. In a 1979 survey of the adult population of the United States, Kuka, Veroff, and Douvan found that 59% of those surveyed reported that they could imagine circumstances under which they might benefit from discussing their psychological problems with someone. Of these, 26% had sought and received some type of psychological help. The 59% reported by Kuka et al. (1979) is double the use rate reported a decade earlier (Gurin, Veroff, & Feld, 1960). In a 1995 *Consumer Reports* survey, use rate for mental health services increased to 31.36% (Consumer Reports, 1995).

The cost of treating these problems is enormous and rising: From 1985 to 1988, treatment costs increased at an average rate of 13.9% per year, and an estimated $273.3 billion was spent in 1988 alone. Of these costs an estimated $2.8 billion was spent in 1985 alone on services of office-based psychologists and counselors, who provided a broad range of psychotherapy services (Dawes, 1994). Dawes estimated that the 1990 costs for these same office-based services alone would be $8.1 billion! The prevalence of the emotional disorders treated by psychological services has increased to the point where most people in our culture now consider them to be a critical social problem (Yankelovitz, 1990).

The tremendous need for and cost of psychological services is straining our health care system. Corresponding attempts to manage both the volume and cost of these services has changed the landscape of professional counseling. One of the main changes is that we have entered an era of accountability. Counselors are, in this new environment, "under the gun" to provide counseling services and to justify their need. Insurance review boards and managed care panels now control whether services are provided, the extent of those services, and many of the fees that fund public and private counseling services. States are cutting mental health budgets and closely monitoring the services they provide. School districts want to know what services students are receiving and the efficiency of those activities. The trend toward accountability is also spreading within some professional organizations. The American Psychological Association has created a task force to consider practice and training guidelines based on empirically validated treatments (Moses-Zirkes, 1993). Clinical practice guidelines are currently being published by the American Psychiatric Association. Thus far, guidelines on eating disorders, depression, and substance use disorders have appeared.

We believe that one source of information to meet the increasing demands for accountability is the knowledge-base that has accumulated during the more than 60 years of counseling outcome research. As we will explore in the succeeding chapters, there is a plethora of counseling outcome studies that have investigated the efficacy of counseling. This information has the potential to be a professional counselor's best friend (Seligman, 1996). Armed with research-based practice guidelines, counselors can make informed arguments to others (e.g., third party-payers, school administrators, potential clients) about the effectiveness of counseling. Research not only provides an indication of the effectiveness of counseling, but also identifies what contributes to successful counseling with specific client problems and psychological disorders. Without systematic research knowledge, it may be increasingly difficult to convince third party payers and the public that counselors can deliver effective and appropriate services.

What is most curious is that although the need for research seems to be growing, there exists a serious split between counseling research and counseling practice. It is a division that many never expected, a split between relying on knowledge gained from systematic empirical inquiry and knowledge resulting from clinical experience. The split is often framed as one between those espousing the art of counseling (intuitive understanding based on clinical experience) and those proposing reliance on the science of counseling (based on systematic study).

Although many propose that counseling is both a science and an art, there is increasing evidence that the science portion of the equation is neglected. The extent of this neglect is illustrated by a number of recent surveys. Among the unfortunate findings is evidence that practitioners do not read research (Morrow-Bradley & Elliot, 1986), engage in research (Norcross, Prochaska, & Gallagher, 1989), and furthermore, that counseling research currently has little or no impact on counseling practice (Anderson & Heppner, 1986; Barlow, 1981; Cohen, Sargent, & Sechrest, 1986; Falvey, 1989; Howard, 1985). In addition, even with the increases in both the quantity and quality of counseling research, there appears to be little evidence that clinicians have adopted a more positive attitude concerning its relevance (Strupp, 1989). Consequently, clinical outcome research is often neglected in favor of strategies based on clinical or personal experiences, clinical training, or therapeutic intuition (Kanfer, 1990).

This gap has serious consequences for the practicing counselor and counselor educator. Without this storehouse of research knowledge the practitioner may not be aware of critical therapeutic findings and, thus, may not provide clients with the best possible services (Marten & Heimberg, 1995). Without research-based knowledge, counselor educators must rely on personal choice, professional preference, or history in determining what to teach aspiring student counselors. Some have also argued that counseling practitioners cannot comply with the ethical code without a thorough knowledge of the counseling research (Lambert, Masters, & Ogles, 1991; Singer, 1980). The ACA's "Code of Ethics and Standards of Practice" (ACA, 1995) states "counselors and their clients work jointly in devising integrated individual counseling plans that offer reasonable promise of success (p. 33)." Without knowledge of outcome studies counselors will have difficulty knowing if intervention or approaches have been shown to be successful. In our current era of increased litigation, counselors who cannot substantiate their treatment selections with research studies are easily sitting ducks for lawsuits. On the pragmatic side, it is also important to note that there are signs that outcome research may soon become one of the primary bases of policy and administrative decisions regarding a broad range of mental health care services (Speer, 1994). Guidelines published by the American Psychiatric Association are already influencing policy makers (APA, 1993a, 1993b; Barlow, 1996). Thus, counselors who lack the necessary empirical knowledge to effectively practice may be viewed as second-class citizens. On a broader professional level, the credibility of the profession could be endangered unless research knowledge becomes an integral part of counselors' clinical decision making and training (Kanfer, 1990).

There are not just external pressures to incorporate research into practice. Effective clinical decision making is a complex process in which professionals must be able to process enormous amounts of information quickly and efficiently. To be effective the knowledge used in clinical decision making must be reliable, valid, and represent the best of what we know about behavior change. Along this line, Wiggins (1992) predicted that research-based practice guidelines are imminent and may soon become the standard for good practice. We believe that most counselors are internally motivated and desire information that will help them intervene more effectively. However, as we have suggested above, there is ample evidence to indicate that counselors do not turn to counseling outcome research for help. Instead, the culture of professional counseling seems to have become one in which clinical outcome research is neglected and ignored in favor of strategies such as intuition, training, or clinical or personal experiences (Kanfer, 1990).

Overcoming the research–practice gap by integrating counseling outcome research into practice is the goal of this book. In talking with colleagues, discussing these issues at conferences, supervising and teaching students, and writing about research, we have come to believe that two major issues stand in the way of that goal: an overreliance on clinical experience and intuition and a series of myths about outcome research. Both of these issues contribute to practitioners' perceptions that outcome research is irrelevant and incompatible with counseling. In our investigations of outcome research we have become convinced that these issues need not separate the profession. We contend that when research and practice are considered as an integrated whole, the criticisms presented in this chapter will no longer be obstacles separating research and practice. In the end, we believe integration can only lead to more effective treatments for the clients seeking our professional help.

Clinical Experience and the Limits of Human Decision Making

Throughout this book we advocate, possibly even plead, for the integration of research and practice. For us, the operative word is *integration*. We firmly believe that both research knowledge and practical experience are necessary for skillful counseling. We endorse the idea that counseling is both a science and an art and that effective counseling involves both factors. However, we frequently attend conferences where the theme is some derivative of the "art of counseling." Presenters view counselors as artists whose decisions come from intuition rooted in clinical experience. We have also attended case staffings where, when asked for a rationale for a clinical decisions, the response is based on personal preference, intuition, or clinical experience. We've heard other counselor educators preach that personal knowledge is paramount to counselor effectiveness and that by knowing oneself one can be an effective helper. Hence, we fear that the balance between the science and art in counseling has been heavily swayed toward art, and science has been completely excluded.

There is growing evidence to support our contention that intuitive and experienced-based judgment cannot be the sole factor in effective decision making. The most persuasive of these arguments focuses on the problems inherent in any human decision making. This literature suggests that as human deciders we are inherently biased in our judgments. Decisional biases exist in a wide variety of contexts—deciding when to buy or sell stock (Johnson, 1988), predicting graduate school success (Dawes, 1979), and estimating the possible failure of a bank (Libby, 1976). Contrary to what practitioners may like to believe, counselors are not immune from decisional bias. A preponderance of evidence suggests that counseling practitioners do an inadequate job of making accurate client diagnoses and behavioral predictions (Dawes, 1986; Dawes, Faust, & Meehl, 1989;

Tracey, 1991). Without exception, statistical regression models are significantly more accurate than clinicians in making accurate clinical judgments (Tracey, 1991).

Further evidence for these claims can be found in the considerable evidence that shows there is little difference between "expert" and "novice" practitioners in diagnosing and predicting client behavior (Johnson, 1988; Tracey, 1991). Experts certainly have more complete representations of counseling, attend to different information, usually process information more quickly, have more extensive strategies for judgments, and are more flexible in applying knowledge. However, even with all of these advantages, experts seem to make the same decision-making errors as novices (Dawes, 1994; Johnson, 1988).

The inherent biases in human decision making center around the problems of selective recall, selective interpretation, and the power of preexisting assumptions (Dawes, 1991). The best way to understand these biases is to consider the heuristic models used to make complex clinical decisions and the way in which reconstructed memory reinforces these decisions. Cognitive heuristics models are the rules that we use to understand the information with which we are presented—they are sets of rules about how to go about solving problems and making sense of clinical situations (Dawes, 1994).

The most common model used in decision making is a comparison model (Tracey, 1991). This deciding rule is one that states that to make sense of any situation, we search our memories for similar situations and use those situations as the basis for our understanding and deciding. The counseling practitioner compares, for example, a current client to former clients of a similar type previously encountered.

The validity of our comparison-based decisions depends on two factors—availability and representativeness. Availability speaks to the sample size we draw on in making our comparisons. Valid decision making requires that we have in our storehouse a wide variety of situations to which we can compare the current situation. Representativeness involves accurately matching characteristics of the current situation with an appropriate category. In accurate decision making we must be able to correctly identify the current situation and then match it appropriately to a suitable category. Furthermore, the number of situations within that category must be of sufficient size to adequately categorize that group of situations. Therefore, our ability to make valid clinical decisions depends on having a large sample of clients that represent all possible problems. Within each problem category (e.g., depression, marital problems, school phobia) we must have a sufficient sample to adequately represent that category. For the comparison model to lead to a good decision we must remember all cases and categories with equal strength, and give equal consideration to each possibility.

Unfortunately, a comparison model commonly leads human deciders to biased judgments (Dawes, 1994; Tracey, 1991). We are all limited in the number of available comparisons—either because of limited experiences, experiences focused more in one area, or a biased memory of these experiences; consequently, we, like other human deciders, make biased comparisons. Unfortunately, when comparing a client to similar clients, it is virtually impossible for the clinician to consider all of the possible variables in determining the correct diagnosis. The inclination for a small sample to be more biased than a large one isn't always taken into account. Furthermore, when using the available sample, human deciders typically attach the same probability to all possible comparisons and, consequently, place the same confidence in judgments of events that are highly probable (what a client will do tomorrow) and those that are significantly less probable (what a client might do in a year). Finally, as for any decider, if a certain client is more salient, a similar category is more easily retrieved from memory. Thus, it is no surprise that counselors see new clients as similar to ones commonly encountered in their practice, predominately use certain diagnosis, and notice that client stories have similar threads.

What makes experience-based clinical decision making even more seductive is that these judgments often feel correct to the clinician. This illusion of accuracy is based on the inherent biases of our memories. The validity of clinical experience is based on the belief that our memory of what occurred with other clients is accurate. Current memory research, however, suggests that memory is a reconstructive process (Loftus, 1993). Instead of remembering the exact details of what happened, we actually make sense out of the bits and pieces of the past by filling in the gaps based on what we think today. Moreover, once we make sense of these traces, our future searches of memory are highly influenced by the way we initially reconstruct the past. Thus, future memory searches tend to become self-fulfilling prophecies in which we remember what we already believe. Dawes (1994) calls this a "hindsight bias," in which we conclude what we knew all along. Thus, the reconstructive nature of memory further enhances the biases already inherent in human decision making and creates the illusions that clinical experience is an unbiased foundation from which to make clinical decisions.

We are not suggesting that experience is not an important and useful source of information for clinical decision making. Instead, we argue that unbalanced experience can, because of the inherent biases, overwhelm logic. Thus, it is a poor exclusive or primary source of guidance for counseling practice. We think counseling outcome research offers a perfect complement to experience. The very weaknesses of experience—availability and representativeness—are the strengths of systematic research.

Myths of Outcome Research

Throughout the history of counseling outcome research there have been criticisms of its goals, methods, and conclusions. These criticisms have served as rationales for practitioners to use in dismissing research as an irrelevant part of clinical decision making. There is no question that outcome research has weaknesses and limitations. Clinicians need to understand these limitations so that they are no longer roadblocks to integrating research into practice. From our work, we have come to the conclusion that although some of the criticisms of outcome research continue to be legitimate, many of the early complaints are no longer valid. In this section we address the common myths associated with outcome research that arise from these criticisms. It is our view that these myths represent tensions inherent in any field of applied research, rather than the incompatibility of research and practice.

Myth 1: Outcome research doesn't provide anything relevant to the practitioner

The perceived irrelevance of outcome research to counseling practice has a long history. In the early days of counseling research many counseling practitioners rightfully perceived outcome research to be based on overly reductionistic questions, and that it used methods that simplified clinical practices, with participants who had little similarity to actual clients (Tracey, 1991). Over the last 10 years researchers responded to these criticisms by studying more relevant questions and using sophisticated research methods (Watkins &

Schneider, 1989). The result is a number of high quality studies performed in multiple settings, using validated treatments, and reliable outcome measures (e.g., Elkin et al., 1989; Shapiro et al., 1994).

Counseling outcome research is, however, an applied area and as such serves two different masters—rigor (the basic research master) and relevance (the utilitarian master). Those in the rigor camp commonly criticize counseling researchers for being soft because they use fuzzy operational definitions and methodologies that have little experimental control. For practitioners, however, those highly controlled studies are too far removed from how counseling is actually done. The constraints necessary to isolate pertinent variables (internal validity) decrease the applicability of actual counseling situations (external validity). Caught in this bind, researchers have often asked simplistic questions and used methods that overly reduce complex clinical situations (Tracey, 1991).

There will probably always be tension between the controls necessary for internal validity and the applicability for external generalization (Gelso, 1979). Gelso suggested that this struggle is somewhat like trying to squeeze an air bubble out from under a window sticker. The more one attempts to push the bubble out the more the bubble moves from one place to another. Any attempt to highly control the variables and attend to the rigor of a study results in loss of usefulness. It may be that, like the window sticker, such flaws cannot totally be eliminated.

Rigor and relevance need not be mutually exclusive concepts. In fact, researchers are beginning to tackle the ways in which psychological research can be both rigorous and relevant. The goal is for researchers to study phenomena in practical settings in ways that permit convincing interpretation of results. In fact, according to Martin and Hoshmand (1995), rigor in outcome research is impossible without relevance. They contend that relevance is a necessary prerequisite for internal validity in counseling outcome research. In our view, the rigor versus relevance dichotomy only succeeds in broadening the gap between research and practice when it doesn't have to.

Myth 2: Research results cannot be trusted

There are currently thousands of studies that use diverse methods and produce a wide array of sometimes contradictory findings. However, a number of current surveys of outcome research literature successfully make the case that, even with the contradictions, there is a large body of research, which investigates many client problems and clinical techniques in various areas of practice, that is potentially useful for practitioners (Francis & Aronson, 1990; Hill, Nutt, & Jackson, 1994).

The best characterization of the current state of outcome research is illustrated by Sexton's (1996) recent survey of the last eight years of published research. In his systematic review of 365 outcome studies published in 116 different journals, he identified 542 different clinical research questions. The most common study in this sample investigated the impact of client characteristics, specific interventions, or theoretical approaches on varying counseling outcomes. Most individual counseling studies explored the efficacy of counseling techniques in treating depression, anxiety, or panic disorders. In career counseling, the largest proportion of studies examined factors that have an impact on career decision making and effective role functioning. Of these studies, most investigated clients' attitudes toward career change as opposed to the accuracy of their self-knowledge or the appropriateness of their career choices. School counseling studies focused equally on evaluating guidance activities and the usefulness of responding to specific student needs with little emphasis on either individual planning or system support interventions. Sexton (1996) also found that a wide range of research methods, each providing different information, are being used to investigate outcomes. The most common outcome study in his review was a clinical trial that used actual clients and practicing counselors in a quantitative analysis that did not include randomized assignment or control group comparisons.

It is clear that given the state of our inquiry methods, no one study has the reliability or validity to serve as the basis of counseling practice. However, taken as a whole, the knowledge base we have accumulated is substantial. Out of this research a number of significant trends have emerged. These trends are based on findings that consistently appear across studies, clients, and settings, and have been replicated often (Orlinsky, Grawe, & Parks, 1994). Section II of this book applies these trends to the various areas in which counselors practice.

Myth 3: Research studies examine minute detail not clinical problems

Being based in the traditions of physical science and logical positivism, outcome researchers have primarily focused on the reduction of elements that comprise clinical practice. The assumption is that by breaking the complex process down into manageable components that can be easily analyzed, these components can later be aggregated to form an understanding of the whole process. Such fine-grained analysis of counseling has certainly provided useful information about the complex phenomena involved in counseling. However, many critics argue that the act of reducing complex social phenomena distorts the very phenomena under study (Hoshmand & Martin, 1995).

These problems are probably no more apparent than in studies of the counseling relationship. Early research efforts sought to find the simple elements that comprise successful relationships between counselors and clients. These efforts led some to claim a whole plethora of conditions to be the core of these relationships. For example, the Rogerian conditions of empathy, genuineness, positive regard, and congruence are often considered to be synonymous with good therapeutic relationships. Unfortunately, most of the time the context in which these conditions were offered was not considered. In the end, attempts to reductionistically study the relationship produced results that were not particularly helpful. And recent research has found the relationship to be significantly more complex than these early discoveries encouraged us to believe (Sexton & Whiston, 1994).

There will probably always be the need for some degree of reduction in the study of counseling processes. However, using an array of complex methods, counseling outcome research has moved out of the laboratory into realistic clinical settings. Researchers now consider broad clinical processes as whole units. As you will see in later chapters, the stage of the counseling process and the match between client and counselor is now a common characteristic of outcome research. Moreover, using sophisticated research review methods (see Chapter 2), researchers are now able to reliably put small discoveries together and identify broad trends relevant to real clinical problems.

Myth 4: Outcome research only looks at group differences; practitioners need help with individual clients

Following the lead of physical science, psychological research has also been primarily concerned with identifying general laws governing groups of individuals—a *nomothetic focus*. Along this line, most outcome studies focus on groups of clients by determining average changes in predetermined process variables. By definition, a nomothetic focus aggregates individual changes into group data. Some suggest that such aggregation results in the loss of the important differences among clients and obscures the stage-like nature of counseling (Kazdin, 1981). Practitioners more often take an *ideographic focus* and recognize that counseling is an individual process in which what happens at the beginning is very different from events that occur near the end of treatment (Tracey, 1993).

The dilemma for researchers is how to identify valid and reliable trends, and still maintain the uniqueness of the individual. Without this balance, we risk developing knowledge that fits everyone to some extent, but no one individual accurately (Martin & Hoshmand, 1995). In addition, we might explain a few individuals comprehensively without useful ways to understand the broader patterns that unite people. A synergistic relationship between research and practitioner and a diversity of quantitative and qualitative research methods are necessary to strike a pragmatic balance.

Myth 5: Research only seeks statistical significance; practitioners need to know what makes a practical difference

With a large enough group of clients even a minute and indistinguishable change can be statistically significant. We have all seen studies that applaud the significant difference between two group of clients who differ only minimally on some outcome measure. Statistical significance does not ensure practical importance. We have yet to develop a universal method for determining how much change is enough to declare a technique or approach effective. However, a number of promising models have been proposed. For example, some researchers now propose that we establish measurable clinical thresholds that can be used to determine when the clients move from dysfunctional to functional levels (Jacobson, Follette, & Revenstorf, 1984). Such movement would constitute a clinically relevant improvement.

Myth 6: Research focuses on evaluating theory; practitioners need clinical discoveries of new methods

Traditional scientific method calls for a theory-testing model of outcome research whose purpose is verification. Research begins with a theory that specifies what is to be investigated and then uses methods that eliminate any extraneous variables. The goal is to verify or test theories in various settings with various clients. The top-down approach of verification research has been criticized by many who suggest that, using this model, we have really learned very little about what actually happens in counseling (Hill, 1982; Mahrer, 1988; Patton, 1989). An alternative aim of research is to discover relevant clinical phenomena that effect outcome. This approach begins with an open-ended study of counseling from which questions and directions emerge as the inquiry process progresses. Nevertheless, this approach is more susceptible to problems of bias (i. e., discovering what you want to know) and generalizability (i. e., discovering factors unique to only one setting).

Dichotomously thinking of research as either verification or discovery oriented only increases the gap in research and practice and is no longer a useful distinction (Martin & Hoshmand, 1995). There is no question that discovery oriented approaches have been neglected, but an abandonment of verification could be equally problematic. Some sort of verification of theories seems necessary if we are to enhance our knowledge of psychological practice. Thus, relevant outcome research must combine discovery and verification using appropriate and systematic methods for each purpose. Moreover, research results from each of these philosophies need to be considered in light of the limitations inherent in each.

Myth 7: Research doesn't provide anything that can be used in practice

There are discrepant expectations of consumers and producers of outcome research. Practitioners often want prescriptive results that are guaranteed to work with the clients sitting across from them. Research, however, is based on assumptions of probability (e.g., what are the chances of finding this result), not certainty. Sometimes the findings are robust and we can have a high degree of confidence in the findings. Other times, the effect sizes are smaller and we can't be as confident. At its best, research is a probabilistic enterprise providing us an indication of the likelihood that something will work.

Given its probabilistic nature, we think it may be more useful to think of the yield of outcome research as being conceptual rather than prescriptive (Martin & Hoshmand, 1995). As such, research findings enhance the general understanding of how a particular intervention might work. Specific step-by-step instructions and exact identification of what to do when, under what conditions (prescriptive), is unlikely. Hoshmand and Martin (1995) offer a "pragmatic framework" for the integration of research and practice (see Chapter 8). Along this line, a useful way to look at outcome research is as a work in progress, in which the trends in the accumulated body of research knowledge rather than any single study, serve as a source of clinical interventions.

Integrating Research Into Practice

The integration of research into practice should be a primary objective of counseling practitioners, educators, and researchers, but there are a number of barriers in the way of such integration. These barriers are apparent in the common criticisms of outcome research presented in this chapter. It is our observation that for the integration of research and practice to proceed, both practitioners and researchers need to understand the interdependent relationship between research and practice that must be at the core of effective and efficient clinical decision making. In such a relationship, the experience of practitioners generates questions as the researcher investigates those questions in a systematic manner. This means practitioners need to become involved by both generating questions and using findings appropriately. Researchers must, in turn, focus on clinically useful questions relevant for clinical practice. We return to the issue of integration in Chapter 8.

One of the ways to continue the integration of research into practice is to make research-based findings a significant part of the counselor education programs. We agree with Peterson (1995), who suggested that it is reasonable to expect that only those procedures shown by careful research to be useful should be taught, and those procedures that have been extensively tested and failed to show usefulness should not. Thus, research needs to be a central component in educational programs and courses. In addition, to become consumers of outcome research, student counselors need an open attitude about integrating research into practice. A new research attitude could be conveyed to the next generation of counselors if training programs would begin helping students become active consumers of outcome research throughout their programs. It is in our training programs that each of us develops many of the habits we continue to follow as professionals. Unfortunately, research is often taught as a generic course in which the basic methods of quantitative methodology are presented in ways that have little relevance to practice. Research education needs to be an integral part of counselor education where students are taught to actively seek research guidance in clinical decisions and are taught relevant research-based practice guidelines. In addition, students should be taught to be action researchers, using systematic research skills to measure their effectiveness in whatever setting they counsel.

The current gap between science and practice only hinders our ability to effectively serve clients. We believe that research findings need to have parity with other sources of information that impact clinical decision making. For that to happen, an understanding of the nature of counseling outcome research is necessary. In the next chapter we look at the guiding questions and methods of counseling outcome research. These questions and methods make up the nature of contemporary counseling outcome research. Section II of the book focuses on the application of outcome research to counseling practice. We are interested in addressing relevant clinical questions—Is it effective?, What makes it effective?, and How can already effective counseling be enhanced? Section III addresses the integration of research into the culture of the counseling profession. Our goal is to identify methods to access research and to provide a pragmatic model of the relationship between research and practice. The aim is a useful model that can be used by practitioners to appropriately consume the available research information and make it a part of ongoing clinical decision making.

CHAPTER 2

The Foundations of Counseling Outcome Research

For outcome research to become a part of clinical decision making, counseling practitioners must have confidence that the findings are relevant, reliable, and valid. We suggest that this belief comes, at least in part, from understanding the nature of outcome research and the extent of the knowledge it has generated. The nature of outcome research is best understood by considering the questions that guide the inquiry process, the common methods used to answer those questions, and the strengths and limitations of these varied approaches. The relationship between inquiry questions and methods is a synergistic one—as new questions develop, new inquiry methods evolve. Likewise, as new research tools come on line, the questions become more complex.

In this chapter we provide a perspective on the applied nature of counseling outcome research. The chapter is not intended to be a research text; instead, it is an overview of the current status of counseling outcome research. This foundation should help practitioners know how to glean the most from the available research. As a backdrop, we first discuss the evolution of counseling outcome research. This evolution is best illustrated by the types of questions that have guided the systematic inquiry of counseling outcomes. Second, we briefly discuss the range of inquiry approaches typically used in outcome studies. Each of these methods has unique strengths and weakness that determine what practitioners can gain from results. In some cases, the study methods may be methodologically weak and we can have little confidence in the results. In other cases, the method is particularly good at providing information that is useful in various clinical situations. Finally, we suggest that matching clinical questions that are relevant to practitioner with the appropriate methods will result in both a sound and useful base of counseling knowledge.

The Evolution of Counseling Outcome Research

Counseling research has a long history. Through time the questions that have guided the inquiry process have become increasingly complex. Likewise, the methods used to answer those questions have become technically advanced. What is important for the consumer of outcome research to remember is that each question and method has both strengths and limitations that mediate the ecological validity of the findings. The appropriate use of the research-based knowledge depends on understanding these questions, methods, and limitations.

Guiding Questions

Three questions have guided the process of the outcome research (Lambert et al., 1991). The first questions asked by outcome researchers concerned the effectiveness of counseling and psychotherapy. The second set of questions attempted to determine the specific factors that influence counseling effectiveness. The final questions focused on identifying methods that may enhance effective counseling. For each question, the researcher used different comparisons and different research methodologies.

Is counseling effective? Counseling effectiveness has been the subject of hundreds of studies. Investigating this basic question has turned out to be amazingly complicated. Early studies of counseling outcome were primarily retrospective and anecdotal accounts reported by practitioners. Initial attempts to systematically study counseling usually involved using some measure before and again after counseling. Unfortunately, simple pre- and postcomparison based studies are not able to factor out critical mediating variables, such as changes that clients make on their own without counseling.

If the effects of counseling in general, or a counseling technique in particular, are no better than a natural healing process, then it really is of no benefit. Eysenck (1952) challenged the early research studies with claims that spontaneous remission rates in untreated patients were identical to those reported by researchers. Eysenck argued that 67% of untreated clients would improve on their own, a rate equal to those early measures of counseling outcome. In response to the problems associated with spontaneous remissions, research designs were improved to include random assignment of clients to either a treatment or nontreatment comparison group. A no-treatment control group accounts for the natural healing process and, therefore, the efficacy of counseling can be more accurately identified.

The issue of spontaneous remission rates is an important one. In an analysis of outcome research, Lambert et al. (1991) concluded that as much as 43% of the improvement clients make is due to factors outside the counseling process. Interestingly, the range of these spontaneous improvement rates varied widely (from 0 to 90%!). Although it is impossible to know why these clients improve, it is important for us to consider the remission process in both our practice and research. We do know that spontaneous remission rates vary depending on the client's disorder. If the client's concern is of short duration and a lesser degree of intensity, spontaneous remission is more frequent (Lambert, 1976; Mann, Jenkins, & Belsey, 1981). Depression has the highest remission rates, followed by anxiety, phobic, and obsessive-compulsive disorders, and remission is more likely if the client has a higher quality social support system, particularly the marital relationship (Lambert et al., 1991). Thus, it seems that spontaneous remission is an active part of the change process, one that follows different courses depending on the difficulty experienced by the client.

Placebo control comparisons are commonly used by researchers attempting to partial out the effects of spontaneous remission. The notion of placebo is borrowed from psychopharmacology research as a method to determine the "active ingredients" in therapy. This type of comparison calls for a control group to account for the nonspecific aspects of treatments that might cause improvement. In medicine, the active ingredients of a drug under study are compared to a condition in which everything except that active ingredient is duplicated.

Subjects in placebo conditions take similar looking pills in identical conditions. The logic is that by controlling these inactive elements, we can better determine the active elements of successful counseling.

Although conceptually appealing, placebo control comparisons are problematic in counseling research. A true placebo condition would be one in which nothing therapeutic exists. Some define placebo condition as one where there is no theoretical base to the therapy provided (Rosenthal & Frank, 1956). Others have suggested that placebos actually represent the nonspecific factors (e.g., relationship between client and counselor) in therapy. In counseling, these nonspecific factors may have a therapeutic effect and, thus, do not represent a true placebo condition. Experience shows that placebo conditions are difficult to create in counseling.

The unique nature of placebo conditions in counseling outcome research is illustrated by the findings of three recent studies. By condensing the results of 15 meta-analyses, Lambert and Bergin (1994) demonstrated that psychotherapy was the most effective condition and that the placebo condition was significantly more effective than a no-treatment comparison. The statistic often used in such studies is effect size (ES). Effect size is an estimate of the magnitude of the relationship between two variables. In the case of outcome research, effect size generally measures the relationship between a treatment and the outcome. Higher effect sizes represent stronger relationships (a more extended discussion of effect size is presented in the section on meta-analysis). Lambert, Weber, and Stykes (1993) found this same pattern of effects. The average psychotherapy clients were better off than those in a no-treatment group (ES = .82) and those in placebo groups (ES = .48). However, the placebo clients were more improved than those in the no-treatment group (ES = .42). Clum (1989) found that psychological treatments of agoraphobia and panic attack problems typically resulted in an approximately 70% improvement, placebo control in a 40% improvement, whereas no-treatment controls resulted in a 30% improvement.

These studies illustrate that counseling clients in placebo conditions improve even though they receive no formal treatment. Thus, placebo controls may be more accurately viewed as "common factors" conditions in which the nontheoretical and common elements of counseling are active (Lambert & Bergin, 1994). In a later section, we will address how outcome research is beginning to identify common elements that are shared by many different counseling approaches. If we can identify the common ingredients that are active in counseling, we may then be able to have placebo conditions that truly lack any therapeutic elements.

What aspects of counseling are helpful? Once we know that counseling or a particular counseling technique is effective, the next logical question is what aspects of that intervention contribute to its success? Three types of strategies have evolved in the search for those elements of counseling that may contribute to effectiveness: differential effectiveness comparisons, process/outcome analyses, and dismantling strategies. Each of these strategies involve different types of comparisons.

Differential effectiveness strategies involve comparisons between various counseling approaches (e.g., "Is dynamic treatment more effective than Gestalt or client-centered therapy?"). A classic study by Sloan, Staples, Cristol, Yorkson, and Whipple (1975) is a good example of a well-conducted investigation using this strategy. Features of their study included a large sample of clients matched according to presenting concern, few client dropouts, random assignment of clients to specifically determined treatment groups, use of multiple outcome measures, and follow-up assessment after a period of time to see if the gains continued. Ninety highly motivated clients were recruited to participate in a comparison of short-term analytically oriented psychotherapy, behavior therapy, and a minimal-treatment wait list control group. After 4 months, all of the treatment groups had improved on the multiple outcome measures (i.e., target complaints, global improvement, and social functioning) when compared to the wait list control group. There were no significant differences between the various treatment groups, other than improvements in social functioning, which favored the behavioral therapy group. At an 8-month follow-up, there was no significant difference between any of the treatment groups, but clients did seem to maintain their improvements.

Process-to-outcome strategies involve comparisons between a class of process variables (e.g., client characteristics, counselor techniques, or some specific intervention) and counseling outcome. In more complex studies, the interaction of variables and the stage of the counseling process are also studied. Process–outcome correlations are intuitively appealing relationships that can make an important contribution toward understanding effective counseling. Such results can, however, be inappropriately applied. For example, some reviews of counseling find counselor empathy to be related to outcome (Sexton & Whiston, 1994). One might conclude, given the robust nature of this finding, that empathy is a predictor of successful outcome (i.e., if the counselor is empathetic, the client will improve). Such conclusions are not necessarily accurate, as these results only represent measures of association, not causality. Thus, the most we can actually say is that counselor empathy seems to be related to successful outcome.

Dismantling strategies study a particular treatment package with an established effectiveness by dismantling it into its component parts. The differential effectiveness of the dismantled components are then compared. Those elements of the program contributing most to successful outcome are retained, and those that do not contribute are eliminated. As an example, consider the panic disorder program developed by Barlow. This program includes relaxation training, cognitive restructuring, and exposure. In a dismantling study, Barlow, Craske, Cerney, and Klosko (1989) compared relaxation training, imaginal exposure plus cognitive restructuring, and a combined treatment (including relaxation, exposure, and restructuring) versus a wait list control. Results from 60 panic disordered clients all showed improvement. At the end of 15 weekly sessions, 36% of the wait list, 60% of the relaxation training, 85% of the exposure and cognitive restructuring, and 87% of the combined group were panic-free. The results of this dismantling study indicate that all three elements of the Barlow protocol should be retained.

How can the effects of effective counseling be enhanced? Given that a counseling approach is effective and that one has identified the elements of that approach that contribute to change, the next logical question is: "What, if anything can we do to further enhance the outcomes?" Studies of this type often match client types with different treatments and match client-counselor characteristics. Matching studies are based on the notion that counseling is generally effective but that not all clients benefit equally from a specific treatment. The assumption is that by matching clients to a particular treatment or process variables researchers can identify the most productive counseling methods for different clients.

There is growing evidence that matching clients, therapists, and treatments may be a crucial factor in enhancing the effects of counseling. For example, Beutler (1989) suggested that client–therapist matching alone may account for as much as 63% of the variance in treatment outcomes. Beutler and Mitchell (1981) compared selected psychoanalytic and experiential procedures with psychiatric outpatients who differed in defensive styles. Sixty percent of the total outcome variance was attributable to the compatibility between the client and therapist. These findings are particularly impressive, given that treatment interventions alone account for only around 10% of outcome variance in counseling outcome. These results would support Luborsky et al.'s (1986) claim that treatment outcome depends more on the client-therapist fit than on the specific type of treatment offered.

Beutler (1989) has proposed a model of dispositional assessment in which these three methods are combined to match various client factors (e.g., interpersonal variables, environmental enabling factors, expectations), therapeutic relationship (similarity, background), therapeutic context (setting, format, duration, and frequency), and aspects of therapeutic interventions. Beutler's (1989) model then proposes three types of client-therapist-treatment matching procedures. The first matches clients with different diagnostic categories to various treatments. The second matches therapists and clients on interpersonal characteristics independent of client diagnosis or therapeutic procedure. The third selectively assigns clients to specific therapeutic procedures based on nondiagnostic client characteristics that seem to fit the demands of the therapeutic procedures (e.g., the ability to self-disclose matched with cathartic oriented procedures).

Approaches to the Study of Counseling Outcomes

Studying counseling outcomes is enormously complex. According to Kazdin (1994), there may be some 400 different approaches to counseling currently in use. In addition, the diagnostic systems (*Diagnostic and Statistical Manual of Mental Disorders,* 4th ed. [*DSM–IV*]; *International Classification of Disorders,* 10th ed. [*ICD–10*]) contain over 300 different client syndromes or disorders. Consider, also, that outcomes might be measured from the perspective of the client, the counselor, or an outside observer. In addition, each might complete numerous possible outcome instruments that measure different target variables. Thus, there is an almost infinite combination of possibilities that the researcher must consider (Kazdin, 1994). Given the complexity of the task, it is no surprise that many practitioners, and even some researchers, are bewildered by process.

We think practitioners can reduce the inherent complexity of outcome research if they have an understanding of the ways in which research attempts to answer its guiding questions. Outcome research methods fall into three primary domains: clinical trials, qualitative reviews of the literature, and meta-analyses. Each methodological domain has advantages and offers unique clinical information. Each also has drawbacks that limit the confidence we might have in the subsequent findings. Our purpose here is to illustrate these methods, what they uniquely offer, and identify the important issues that mediate their contribution to clinical practice.

Clinical Trials

Clinical trials are usually experiments that use one of the comparison methods outlined in the previous section. They are typically based on traditional quantitative research designs in which the researcher observes changes in groups of subjects, some of whom are exposed to the variable of interest (e.g., counseling technique, counselor characteristic) and some of whom are not. Kazdin (1994) suggested that one way to make practical sense of trials is to consider the various types of studies (true experimental, quasi experimental, observational, and naturalistic), combined with three design *strategies* (groups, single groups, and single case) as they take place within certain *settings*. Using Kazdin's scheme, good clinical trials use actual clients in realistic clinical settings, and the clients are treated by common psychological techniques. When well designed, the study adequately controls for many extraneous variables without significantly limiting external validity. As these studies typically occur in actual clinical settings, they mirror the natural complexities of counseling and psychotherapy.

Given the inherent difficulties in outcome research, clinical trial studies are never perfect. The confidence we can have in the findings of a clinical trial study depends on the degree to which it is methodologically reliable and valid. For clinical trial studies, methodological validity requires attention to three important issues. Only by understanding these potential limitations will the consumer be able to weigh the findings presented in the studies reported in Section II.

Appropriate comparison groups. Selecting an appropriate client group is imperative if the findings are to be generalized to counseling practice. The ideal comparison group is one that does not differ from the treatment group in any significant way. Making comparison groups similar is more difficult to achieve than it may seem. Two strategies are typically used in establishing comparison groups—nonclient comparisons and treatment-control groups. Regardless of the approach, comparison groups can differ from those treated in many subtle ways that will impact the applicability of any findings.

Some counseling research studies use people who are not clients as comparisons. Here, individuals who have not asked for counseling are given the same measures as those receiving the treatment, and change is determined by the difference between these groups. There are problems with using nonclients instead of actual clients receiving counseling as a comparison group (Kazdin, 1986). For example, nonclient volunteers will probably not be having as much difficulty as are actual counseling clients. Furthermore, those participants that volunteer may have motives for their involvement in the study that set them apart from clients in important ways.

A second strategy uses a subset of clients who seek counseling as a comparison. This is typically accomplished in two ways. First, clients who are on a waiting list are asked to take the outcome measures. The determination of who is treated now and who remains on the waiting list is made by assessing which are less serious and capable of waiting for treatment. Other times, the comparison group is composed of those clients who drop out of or refuse counseling. Using dropouts as a no-treatment control group is problematic because many of these people are helped by family, friends, and clergy. For example, Bergin (1971) found that as many as 50% of persons seeking formal therapeutic help had sought help from other sources.

Regardless of the strategy (wait list or dropout), the major issue is whether these groups are experiencing the same problem in the same way and at the same level of severity. To ensure comparability, some studies describe the symptom pattern of clients by determining the applicable DSM-IV diagnosis. Unfortunately, although helpful, many DSM diagnoses represent only general clusters of symptoms and do not guarantee similarity. Other studies develop explicit criteria to ensure that clients in their studies are experiencing the same problem at the same level of severity. A study by Williams (1985) illustrated the difficulty in both of these strategies. Williams investigated the diversity of symptom profiles with a seemingly well defined and distinct client problem (agoraphobia). Using DSM III-R criteria, Williams found that the symptom configuration of fears was extremely diverse. In fact, he suggested that no two agoraphobics had the same pattern of fears. In addition, their phobias were very similar to other anxiety-based diagnoses (i.e., generalized anxiety disorder and social phobias).

The nature of the comparison and treatment groups is a critical component of outcome study methodology. Establishing comparable groups is an intricate process. Each method seems to have practical and methodological limitations that should be considered in interpreting the results for clinical practice.

Treatment integrity. If we are interested in measuring the efficacy of a counseling technique or approach, a prerequisite is that the treatment being studied is carried out as it was intended to be practiced (Yeaton & Sechreist, 1981). Unfortunately, many times the label a counselor may use to describe his or her work may be quite different from his or her actual behavior. Thus, good studies need to ensure, through training, supervision, and observation of the counselor, that the technique was performed as intended. Willis, Faither, and Snyder (1987) suggested that treatment integrity can be measured by (a) judging randomly selected session tapes for adherence to the intended method, (b) client report of the events that took place in therapy, or (c) observation of an outside observer. The intent of each method is to see if the variation in administration of the treatment falls within an acceptable range.

Treatment manuals are an increasingly common method to ensure treatment integrity. These written manuals currently cover a wide variety of psychological treatments (for more information, see Lambert & Ogles, 1988). Each manual seeks to operationalize the practice and procedures of an approach (e.g., behavioral, cognitive, family, interpersonal, etc.). Treatment manuals are helpful, but they cannot control for all of the possible intervening variables. They cannot, for example, account for the aspects of the interpersonal relationship or match of personal styles between client and counselors.

The importance of ensuring treatment integrity can be illustrated by considering a common interpretation of a consistent research finding. Numerous clinical trials and reviews have concluded that different counseling approaches or theories are relatively equivalent (Bergin & Garfield, 1994; Stiles, Shapiro, & Elliott, 1986). Unfortunately, in many cases the individual studies that led to this conclusion did little to ensure that the treatments provided were: (a) representative of the intended clinical procedure, (b) conducted for the appropriate duration, or (c) implemented with the necessary intensity (Kazdin, 1994). Consequently, because treatment integrity was not ensured, the equivalence finding, now a common conclusion, may be as much a methodological artifact as a practical difference.

Outcome measures. Effectively measuring client change is central to determining outcome effectiveness. In the early days of outcome research, many counselors were justifiably critical of the simplistic measures used to measure the complex process of client change. We now know that effective outcome measurement involves three major issues: (a) what to measure, (b) the perspective from which to measure the change, and (c) individual versus group change criteria.

Throughout the history of outcome research there has been a debate regarding what measures are adequate representations of clinical outcomes. Measures commonly focus on the reduction of symptoms, improvement in psychosocial functioning, and client satisfaction with the treatment offered. A recent study by Connolly and Strupp (1996) did a cluster analysis of clients' ratings of important therapy outcomes. They found four distinct clusters that accounted for the changes made by clients in the study: improved symptoms, improved self-understanding, improved self-confidence, and greater self-definition. They suggest that a complete battery of outcome measures involve both symptom changes and measures of self-concept change. Significant changes in these areas may have very different implications and potentially contradictory findings. Client satisfaction, for example, could be high but symptom change could be unchanged. There is general consensus that it takes each of these domains to gain a clear picture of the outcome.

Another area of debate concerns whose perspective (client, counselor, or outside observer) to use in outcome measurement. It is now common practice to measure counseling outcomes from multiple perspectives (Lambert, 1983). The use of multiple perspectives is supported by the finding that the outcome of counseling depends on whether the effects are judged by the client, the counselor, or an independent rater (Kazdin, 1980; Orlinsky & Howard, 1986). Although the notion of multiple perspectives is widely accepted, the relative value of these perspectives continues to be debated. Are clients the best evaluators of change, as it is their subjective experience being investigated? Or are outside observers the best judge of change because they are "objective"?

Finally, the nature of change (individual vs. group) is an issue in outcome measurement. Typically, researchers identify an a priori list of outcomes and apply the measures to participants in the study. Because change is averaged across heterogeneous clients, therapists, and settings, the individual nature of the client under study may be lost (Lambert, Shapiro, & Bergin, 1986). Persons (1991) noted that such standardization may actually obscure treatment differences. On the other hand, the use of individualized outcome criteria, although desirable, is more difficult and has reliability problems (Calsyn & Davidson, 1978).

The issue of outcome perspective is well illustrated in a study by Green, Gleser, Stone, and Siefert (1975). They found that the type of rating scale used in a study had more to do with the measures of improvement than the treatment under study. When clients and therapists rated global change, all clients in the study showed significant improvement. However, when they rated specific symptoms, an intensification of some symptoms was more common. In their study, both the perspective and the specificity of the outcome measure were a critical mediating factor in measuring change.

Even though there has been significant progress in the quality of outcome instruments, Lambert and Hill (1994) contend that there is a significant lack of agreement over what is an adequate outcome measure. This problem is illustrated by Froyd and Lambert (1989), who reviewed 348 different outcome studies in which a total of 1,430 different outcome measures were used. Of those, 840 were used only once. Ogles, Lambert, Weight, and Payne (1990) did a similar review of studies in a well-defined problem area, agoraphobia. They found that of the studies, 98 different types of outcome measures were used to study agoraphobia. The same problems even occur in something as quantifiable as the variable "drug use." Wells, Hawkins, and Catalano (1988) identified five different categories of drug use and 25 different procedures for measuring these categories. Sexton (1996) found 297 different measures used 541 times in 258 clinical trial studies. Of these, half were developed by authors for use in their study. There is no question that the nature of the outcome measure is an important factor to consider when using research results.

An impressive example of a large scale clinical trial that addresses these methodological issues is the National Institute of Mental Health (NIMH) Collaborative Depression study (Elkin et al., 1989). This study illustrates the practical methods for addressing complicated methodological issues. Each of the 250 clients in the study met the specific inclusion criteria for depression as measured by the Research Diagnostic Criteria for a major depressive episode and a preset score on the Hamilton Rating scale for depression. Clients were randomly assigned to four treatments offered at various sites around the country. Twenty-eight psychiatrists and psychologists were carefully selected, trained, and monitored. Each therapist saw between 1 and 11 clients and used carefully defined procedures that represented the particular treatment. Treatment manuals included theoretical issues, strategies, major techniques, and procedures to manage typical clinical problems. Treatments were designed to last between 16 and 20 weeks. The study compared a standard reference treatment (imipramine plus clinical management) with cognitive behavioral therapy and interpersonal therapy (a variation of dynamic and humanistic therapy). Furthermore, these three groups were compared to a drug placebo plus clinical management control group. Multiple outcome measures including symptom change and general adjustment were used. These outcomes were measured from multiple perspectives (e.g., client, therapist, and outside observer).

Results indicated that both specific therapies (interpersonal and cognitive-behavioral therapy) resulted in client improvement, but neither was significantly more effective than the placebo plus clinical management control group (Elkin et al., 1989). In addition, no significant differences were found between either of the psychological treatments. When the level of severity of depressive symptoms was accounted for, some differences were found. The most severely depressed patients improved more with interpersonal therapy when compared to the placebo group. Effect sizes for these comparisons were, however, very small. In addition, some sites showed significant improvements for cognitive therapy not evident at other sites.

Qualitative Research Reviews

A second major approach to the study of counseling outcomes involves the systematic review of a number of studies in an area in order to determine useful trends. There are two primary types of systematic literature reviews: qualitative reviews and meta-analysis. Unlike clinical trials, research reviews have the advantage of identifying trends across clients, situations, and studies.

The primary purpose of an integrative qualitative research review is to synthesize the current literature to identify robust trends that are evident across a variety of individual studies. For the practitioner, these reviews, when systematic, can synthesize outcome results so that relevant clinical guidelines can easily be identified. Like all other methods, literature reviews can fall short of the critical criteria necessary to provide valid findings and trends (Cooper, 1982).

Cooper (1982) suggested that integrated research should be seen as a systematic data-gathering process that follows established principles of research design. In counseling outcome research, there are high quality reviews that provide valuable practice guidelines as well as others that are unsound and slanted. Ellis (1991) suggested criteria to ensure that a qualitative review is unbiased and systematic. First, the review must have a formulated rationale and need. Second, the sampling of studies to be included must be based on a clearly delineated operational definition that forms specific inclusion and exclusion criteria to be used in selecting appropriate studies. In addition, the quality of the studies must be evaluated and trends weighted according to the methodological quality of the study.

One of the best examples of a well-designed qualitative research review was conducted by Orlinsky et al. (1994). Their review clearly defined the operational definition of the independent and dependent variables. They identified important issues (e.g., outcome measure, perspective of change) that need to be considered prior to conducting their analysis. They developed a generic psychotherapy model to guide and organize their review, and also set a specific effect size as the criteria for inclusion as an important finding. Most impressive is the breadth of this review. Orlinsky et al. (1994) reviewed all of the available outcome research that focused on process-outcome questions from 1950 to 1992. In these studies, they identified 2,354 different findings. Their review added to the data they presented in a 1986 review. Since 1985, an additional 192 studies published in 46 journals and 13 books have been added to their previous database

Meta-analysis

Meta-anlysis is a quantitative approach to the systematic review of research literature. This technique allows for the data from numerous distinct studies to be combined and statistically averaged so that significant trends can be identified. The resulting statistical indicator, effect size, is the mean differences between the treated and the control subjects divided by the standard deviation of the control group (the specific formula for effect size calculation varies according to the particular method; for a complete discussion see Rosenthal, 1994). Estimates of effect size allow for the determination of the magnitude of difference between the combined treatment and control groups. Meta-analyses share many of the advantages of qualitative reviews. In addition, meta-analysis has the advantage of combining large groups of studies, thus increasing statistical power. Consequently, these studies have the potential to overcome some of the methodological problems contained in any one study.

Brown (1987) suggested that there are three main concerns to be taken into account when using meta-analytic results. First, because meta-analytic procedures are a group of statistical procedures, they are susceptible to violations of assumptions of independence, or problems of *statistical validity*. Second, flaws in individual studies included in the meta-analysis may be obscured in the effect size calculations, thus raising questions about the *methodological validity*. The value of meta-analysis studies depends on the validity of the studies included in the review. Kazdin (1983) suggested that meta-analyses include only studies that meet the highest standards of methodological relevance and clinical relevance. The final concern centers on the generalizability of the meta-analytic findings, or the *conceptual validity*. Like clinical trial research, meta-analytic research is subject to sample biases. On the broadest level, the results of any meta-study depend on all available studies being included.

Psychotherapy was one of the earliest areas to which meta-analysis techniques were applied. In their classic study, Smith and Glass (1977) analyzed 375 studies containing 833 different comparisons of treatment and control group differences. These studies represented approximately 50,000 clients in both clinical and analog studies. The mean therapist experience was 3.5 years, and the average duration of therapy was 17 hours. The influence of 16 different independent variables (e.g., duration of therapy, mode of therapy, therapist experience, type of outcome measure) were calculated. The mean effect size was .85, suggesting that the average client was 75% better off than an untreated control. Interestingly, Smith and Glass found only 10% of the outcome could be attributed to the type of therapeutic approach. The widespread use of meta-analytic procedures will become evident in other chapters of this book.

As a classic study, Smith and Glass's has become the standard with which counseling outcome is measured. It also illustrates the validity problems inherent in meta-analytic work. For example, Miller and Bermen (1983) criticized Smith and Glass's (1977) meta-analysis for failing to include 23 different studies of behavior therapy treatment. Others have criticized meta-analytic studies for relying only on published studies of counseling outcome. Unfortunately, research that is not statistically significant rarely is published. In using meta-analytic results, it is important to evaluate all of these possible threats to validity.

Using Counseling Research in Clinical Decision Making

The questions and methods of outcome research identified in this chapter are designed to serve as a foundation for the integration of research into practice. We argue that outcome research can be applicable to clinical practice when the features of research outlined in this chapter are taken into account. We suggest that it is only when clinical questions are matched with relevant methods, and the limitations of these methods are considered, that outcome research can make an important addition to effective clinical decision making.

Most practitioners can ask two general questions about their clinical practice: What about my work is helpful in producing successful client outcomes? and How can my work be further enhanced? The practitioner can turn to the large number of qualitative and quantitative (meta-analytic) reviews of the research to determine if what they do has been consistently found to be effective. Clinical activities such as how a counselor typically establishes a therapeutic relationship, how sessions are structured, length of treatment, or particular broad categories of counseling interventions can all be validated against the outcome research. The chapters in Section II of this volume address these broad issues.

Counselors can also use the research when considering particular approaches for specific clinical situations. When beginning with a client, the first question is, What might work with this type of client? In another form, the question might be, What combination of clinical structures and techniques will be most effective in helping this particular client problem? Many clients' concerns are well researched and the results of studies have been accumulated in meta-analytic and qualitative reviews. If a qualitative review is used, the systematic nature of the literature search should be evaluated to determine the level of confidence one can have in the findings. If a meta-analysis is the source of guidance, both statistical and methodological validity should be considered. If the reviews meet the methodological criteria identified here, considerable confidence can be given to the results.

The second important question is whether this technique will work for the particular client with which the counselor is working. Because this is a more specific question, clinical trial studies that use similar clients are probably the best source for guidance. With clinical trials, one should consider the nature of the comparison group, issues of treatment integrity, and design sensitivity. Particular note should be made of the way in which significant change is defined. Once the active components are identified and the treatment refined, the next relevant question is usually, How might we match various client, counselor, and treatment factors to create a mix that maximizes effectiveness? Once again, broad trends are best found in reviews, specific results in clinical trials. If the methodological factors have been addressed, one can have confidence in the results. One of the major reasons to be well versed in the methodological issues presented in this chapter is to be able to determine when an area of client concern is well represented in the literature. If the research does not measure up either qualitatively or quantitatively, the practitioner needs to be more cautious in implementing these results.

Effective Counseling
From an Outcome Research
Perspective

CHAPTER 3

How Well
Does Counseling
Work?

A number of consistent and stable findings have emerged from the nearly six decades of study into the effectiveness of counseling. Orlinsky et al. (1994) suggested that these cumulative research results represent trends so often replicated that they may now be "established facts." The majority of this research has been conducted in the area of individual counseling, but many of the results are relevant to the common behavior change processes evident in a wide variety of counseling methods. Counselors, regardless of their settings, work as behavior change agents within the context of therapeutic relationships that share common elements and processes. Therefore, many of these trends also apply across the range of settings in which counseling is the vehicle for behavior change. Considering the robust nature of some of these trends, we believe that it is now essential that they are incorporated into counseling practice and education.

The purpose of this chapter is to identify the empirical basis for the effectiveness of counseling. Our focus is on the range of studies that answer these questions: How effective is counseling (how well does counseling work, how long does it take, and how long does it last)?, Which therapeutic approaches work and which are most effective?, and What are the effective common elements related to successful counseling? To further the discussion of common factors, we also developed a process-based model that will serve as the organizational scheme for the following three chapters. The chapter concludes with implications of these research findings for counseling practice and education.

How Well Does it Work, How Long Does it Take, How Long Does it Last?

In the current era of accountability and managed care, the question of whether counseling is effective is paramount. A number of equally important questions naturally evolve from the issue of effectiveness, such as: To what degree is it effective?, How long does it take?, Who drops out and who stays in?, How long does it last?, and Are there negative effects?"

Does Counseling Work?

One of the most consistent and reliable findings to emerge from both clinical trial and meta-analytic studies is that counseling is a process from which most clients do benefit. The positive effects are above and beyond those associated with the natural healing process (spontaneous remission). These findings are so consistent that Lambert and Bergin (1994) suggested that there is now little doubt that counseling is beneficial.

The first source of evidence for the effectiveness of counseling comes from clinical trial studies. A classic study by Sloan et al. (1975) illustrated how an outcome study can overcome the complex methodological problems identified in Chapter 2 and address the question of counseling effectiveness. Sloane and colleagues were able to adequately sample relevant clients, establish treatments with measured levels of treatment integrity, and use multiple outcome measures. They studied 90 outpatient clients classified as neurotic, who were receiving behavioral and short-term analytically oriented psychotherapy. These clients were compared to both a minimal-treatment and a wait list control group. The researchers trained therapists in their respective approaches and took steps to ensure treatment integrity. After 4 months of treatment, all four groups (analytic, behavioral, minimal treatment, and wait list) had improved on the outcome measure of target symptoms. Those clients treated with the psychological treatments improved significantly more than those in the control groups. Furthermore, these results were maintained at an 8-month follow-up.

A more recent clinical trial conducted by the NIMH Collaborative Depression study used clients and therapists from multiple sites around the country (Elkin et al., 1989). To address the important methodological issues, they used manual-based procedures to ensure treatment integrity, carefully determined client diagnosis to control for client variability, and multiple outcome assessments measured from various perspectives. Two psychological therapies, interpersonal and cognitive-behavioral, were contrasted with a medication placebo plus clinical management treatment. Each of the two therapies were effective (outcome measures were higher than the placebo group alone); however, neither was any more effective than the placebo plus clinical management condition. These results led these researchers to conclude the existence of some set of common factors operating in all three groups. As will be discussed later in the chapter, *common factors* is a term used to describe active elements of counseling that are shared by all theoretical approaches.

A second source of support for the effectiveness of counseling can be found in the growing number of meta-analytic studies. As indicated in Chapter 2, meta-analytic reviews have the advantage of pulling together findings from various studies. Large sample sizes in various settings have been combined to address the question of therapeutic effectiveness. As with clinical trial studies, early meta-analytic review focused exclusively on the efficacy of counseling in general. More recent reviews have focused on what contributes to that effectiveness.

The first major meta-analysis regarding psychotherapy outcome was conducted by Smith and Glass (1977). Their analysis included 475 controlled outcome studies, finding an average effect size for psychotherapy to be .85. Other meta-analyses have found similar improvement rates. Lambert, Shapiro, et al. (1986) and Howard, Kopta, Krause, and Orlinsky (1986) both demonstrated that improvement rates for those clients undergoing psychotherapy was at least 70%, whereas the improvement rate for untreated clients was approximately 40%. Asay, Lambert, Christensen, and Beutler (1984) studied 2,045 clients from various locations exposed to a variety of treatments. They found the average effect size as the result of counseling to be .92. Using .50 standard deviation units as the cutoff score for defining those clients who were improved, they found 66% of clients were considered improved, 26% unchanged, and 8% worse.

These general findings are confirmed by a recent large scale survey of counseling consumers. In collaboration with Martin Seligman, *Consumer Reports* (1995) surveyed their readers about their experiences with emotional problems and counseling. Of *Consumer Reports'* 4 million readers, 184,000 were randomly selected to receive a mental health survey. Of these, 22,000 responded (13%). Of these respondents, 6,900 reported that they had sought help for psychological problems; 900 reported seeking help from mental health professionals. Of the *Consumer Report* readers who sought professional mental health assistance, 43% reported feeling either "very poorly" of "poorly" when they began treatment. The most frequently cited problems included depression, followed by marital or sexual problems, general anxiety, frequent low moods, and problems with children or other family members.

The treatments received were generally viewed as positive. Nine out of ten respondents reported that they were helped with the specific problems that motivated them to seek help. Most (62%) reported feeling "very" or "completely" satisfied with their treatment, 27% reported being "fairly well satisfied," and 11% reported dissatisfaction. Those who started out feeling the worst reported making the most progress. It is important to note that this report was a survey of readers and, thus, has serious methodological problems. For example, we don't know if the sample is representative, the nature of the therapy received, or the skillfulness of the therapist.

How Long Does it Take?

How much is enough is a complex question that, although often studied, has yet to be completely answered. Luborsky, Crits-Christoph, Mintz, and Auerbach (1988) found that the number of sessions was positively related to greater client improvement. On the other hand, in their meta-analysis, Smith, Glass, and Miller (1980) identified a curvilinear relationship between the number of sessions and outcome. Based on a qualitative review, Orlinsky et al. (1994) suggested that, in general, more therapy was probably better, but the relationship is hardly linear. In one of the most complete reports, Howard et al. (1986) studied 2,431 different clients in studies across 30 years. They identified a stable but curvilinear relationship in which 50% of the improvement occurred by the 8th session, 75% occurred by the end of 26 sessions (6 months of once-a-week therapy), and 85% of improvement occurred by the end of the first year (of weekly counseling sessions). These data are supported by a recent analysis of client session-by-session progress (Kadera, Lambert, & Andrews, 1996). Figure 3.1 is a graph of the recovery course for those clients who were judged as having successful outcomes. What seems clear from these recent reports is that much of the impact of therapy occurs relatively early in the process.

A recent study helps sort out the conflicting results concerning the optimal length of counseling. Comparing dynamic and cognitive behavioral treatments of depressions, Shapiro, Barkham, Hardy, and Morrison (1990) found that clients with mild and moderate depression scores did as well in 8 sessions as in 16. Those clients with more severe initial depression scores improved more over 16 than 8 sessions. Furthermore, the differences between these groups widened at the 3-month follow-up. Based on their qualitative review, Lambert and Bergin (1994) suggested that the most effective therapy duration depends on the level of client disturbance, whereas Kopta, Howard, Lowry, and Beutler (1994) suggested that different symptom clusters improve at

Figure 3.1 *Recovery percentage by number of sessions.*

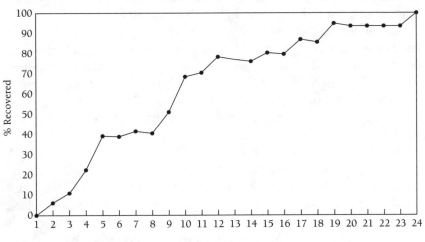

Number of Sessions

Note: From "How much therapy is really enough: A session-by-session analysis of the psychotherapy dose-effect relationship," by S. W. Kadera, M. J. Lambert, and A. A. Andrews, 1996, *Journal of Psychotherapy: Practice and Research,* 5, p. 10. Copyright 1996 by the American Psychiatric Press. Reprinted with permission.

different rates during different phases of treatment. In the *Consumer Reports* survey, Seligman (1996) found that respondents found longer term therapy (2 years) more satisfying than therapy over a shorter term. However, when satisfaction rates are graphed into a does-rate relationship, the results are similar to those reported by Howard et al. (1986). Thus, the effects of therapy may be relatively quick, but the nature of the client concern is an important mediating factor. In any case, we cannot defend the claim that "more is always better."

Who Begins, Who Stays, and Who Drops Out of Counseling?

Counseling can only be effective if a client begins and continues counseling for some period of time. However, the available data shows that of the clients who begin counseling, most remain for only a few sessions. This common pattern is evident in various clinical settings, across patients with diverse disorders, and across various therapeutic modalities. In reviewing meta-analytic reports, Garfield (1994) found that the majority of clients who enter therapy terminate by the 8th session, with a range from 3 to 13 sessions. In a qualitative review, Howard et al. (1986) found that the median number of sessions was 12, with a range of 4 to 33. These data are also confirmed by data from the NIMH collaborative study, where the clients who became involved were highly motivated, expressed a strong desire for counseling, met a systematic screening procedure, were in need of service, and had gone to the trouble to become part of a complex research study. Despite what would seem to be high motivation, between 23% and 30% of clients in each treatment group dropped out prior to completing therapy (Elkin et al., 1989).

A number of client surveys also support these findings. An NIMH survey of 350,000 children and youth involved in mental health services found that 69% had 5 or fewer visits, with only 12.5% continuing beyond 10 sessions. In a survey of private practice psychologists and psychiatrists, 44% of the clients made fewer than 4 visits, and 16.2% of the sample made more than 24 visits. These clients however, accounted for 57.4% of the expense of services (Howard, Davidson, O'Mahoney, Orlinsky, & Brown, 1989) .

A series of correlational studies have been conducted to attempt to understand the differences between potential clients who do not enter, clients who drop out, and clients who complete counseling. An early hypothesis was that the socioeconomic status of the client was related to dropping out. A number of studies did find that lower income clients are less likely to remain in therapy (Garfield & Bergin, 1971; Pilkonis, Imber, Lewis, & Rubinsky, 1984). Lower income clients were also found to miss more sessions in outpatient clinics, and the number of missed sessions was highly related to premature termination (Weighill, Hodge, & Peck, 1983). However, as Garfield (1994) noted, social class is not a unidimensional construct and may also include education (Garfield, 1986), occupation (DuBrin & Zastowny, 1988), expectancy for success (Rabin, Kaslow, & Rehm, 1985), and racial identity (Garfield, 1994).

Demographic characteristics of clients have also been studied. Educational level seems to be related to length of time in counseling and occupation and educational level to be significantly correlated with dropout rates (Dubrin & Zastowny, 1988). The higher the educational level, the longer the time a client is likely to remain in counseling. A host of other client variables, including age (Garfield & Bergin, 1971), client diagnosis (Garfield, 1986), and gender (DuBrin & Zastowny, 1988; Sledge, Moras, Hartley, & Levine, 1990), have been studied but do not seem to be related to early dropout.

Client race plays a part in distinguishing dropouts from continuers, but the results should not be interpreted simplistically. It seems that African American clients are more likely than White clients to terminate early from counseling. Sue, McKinney, Allen, and Hall (1974) found that African American clients at a community mental health center had significantly fewer sessions and discontinued therapy after intake more frequently than did White clients. Sue, Fujino, Hu, Takeuchi, and Zane (1991) conducted a large-scale study of community mental health services and ethnic minority groups. According to their results, Asian Americans and Mexican Americans were underrepresented in the use of mental health services, but African Americans overused services. Ethnic mismatch between client and counselor was related to premature termination for all groups. Atkinson, Furlong, and Poston (1986) studied preferences of African American college students concerning counselor characteristics and found that race was significantly less important than the counselors' level of education and age, and any similarity between the client's and counselor's values, attitudes, and personality. Another recent study also found no significant differences between those who dropped out and those who continued because of the counselor's race (Sledge et al., 1990).

What we do in initial counseling sessions may also contribute to the drop-out rate. For example, clients who complete psychological evaluations are more likely to continue compared to those who do not (Koran & Costell, 1973; Wirt, 1967). Interestingly, the results of these arduous tests are still unable to predict which clients will drop out. Those clients that perceive their therapists to be competent and trustworthy are more likely to continue than those who do not (Kokotovic & Tracey, 1987; McNeill, May, & Lee, 1987). Clients who view their therapist as skillful also seem to continue more often than do clients who question the skillfulness of the therapist (Baekland & Lundwall, 1975; Dodd, 1970; Sloan et al., 1975). Mohl, Martinez, Ticknor, Huang, and Cordell (1991) found that those clients who dropped out early liked their therapist less, felt less respected, experienced a weaker alliance, and perceived the counselor as more passive than did those clients who continued. Tracey (1986) suggested that those client-counselor dyads that continue past the first few sessions can be predicted by the degree to which they mutually agree on definitions of what each is to do. Tracey's work would suggest that whether clients continue in counseling is directly related to the strength and the nature of the working alliance.

It is important to remember that outcome research is primarily based on studies investigating clients who voluntarily begin, follow through with, and successfully terminate counseling. Unfortunately, many clients do not seek counseling voluntarily, but are referred from other sources. Others refuse to even begin therapy once they are referred. Phillips and Fagen (1982), for example, found that almost 49% of clients referred for counseling never come to the first session. There are two important implications of this unfortunate situation. First, we need to realize that outcome research represents only a subset of clients. We do not know much about the group that does not enter counseling, many of whom have similar problems but different motivation or circumstances. Second, the way we deliver services may suit some potential clients much better than others.

Do the Positive Effects of Counseling Last?

It is becoming increasingly clear that the benefits of counseling are not just short-term; these positive changes are generally maintained at a relatively equal rate over the long run (Lambert & Bergin, 1994;

Lambert & Cattani-Thompson, 1996). This conclusion is supported by both clinical trial studies and meta-analytic reviews. Nicholson and Berman (1983) included 67 studies in the meta-analysis of psychotherapy. Studying mostly verbal therapies across a wide range of clients, they found posttherapy results to be significantly correlated with the degree of change at long-term follow-up. Similar results were reported by Jorm (1989), who studied test anxiety treatment in a meta-analysis. Once again, significant treatment results were maintained at a one-year follow up. Numerous studies have indicated that counseling can have an enduring effect in the treatment of depression (Gallagher-Thompson, Hanley-Peterson, & Thompson, 1990; Nietzel, Russel, Hemmings, & Gretten, 1987; Robinson, Berman, & Neimeyer, 1990). Of those clients who were depression free at the end of therapy, 83% remained so at a one-year follow-up and 77% at a two-year follow-up.

Although the maintenance of treatment gains seems impressive, all clients do not remain symptom-free. An important factor differentiating who does maintain change is the degree to which both clients and therapist attribute the changes to the client. For example, those clients who attributed change to themselves maintain change better than those who attributed it to their medication (Frank, 1976; Liberman, 1978). This research suggests that maintaining changes and preventing relapse is based on increased levels of client self-efficacy. Lambert and Bergin (1994) suggested that these findings imply that termination is an important part of the therapy process. Thus, a comprehensive view of therapy would include a treatment phase (phase in which behaviors are changed) and a maintenance stage (stage in which generalization and maintenance strategies are the focus).

Can Counseling be Harmful?

At the current time, it seems apparent that counseling is not a benign activity, and some clients do get worse. The reported rate of clients suffering negative effects ranges from 6% (Orlinsky & Howard, 1980) to 11.3% (Shapiro & Shapiro, 1982), with other researchers documenting negative effects in the same range (Bergin & Lambert, 1978; Beutler, Frank, Schieber, Calvert, & Gaines, 1984; Henry, Schacht, & Strupp, 1986). The source of these negative effects has received little specific attention in the research literature. What we do know is that these negative effects cannot be attributed solely to the therapeutic process or client diagnosis (Luborsky et al., 1986).

One documented source of potential client deterioration is the therapist. For example, across many of the outcome research studies some therapists consistently produced the majority of successful cases, and a few others accounted for the negative effects (Orlinsky & Howard, 1980). Luborsky, McLellan, Woody, O'Brien, and Auerbach (1985) suggested that these different outcomes were attributable to the therapist's skill, the nature of the treatment offered, and the quality of the client–therapist interaction. Luborsky et al. (1985) investigated the differential effects of nine therapists working with opiate-dependent males undergoing different psychological treatments. The therapists were trained in the prescribed treatment and their work was monitored and supervised. The authors noted significant differences in client success rates among the nine therapists, despite the training and supervision. Sachs (1983) found that a number of therapist "errors" could account for a significant degree of negative outcome. In his study, negative effects were accounted for by the counselor's failure to focus or structure the session, failure to address the client's negative attitude toward therapy or the therapist, passive acceptance of the client's resistant and evasive behavior, and poorly timed and inappropriate interventions.

Negative outcomes can also be accounted for by what Lambert and Bergin (1994) call client-technique interaction effects. It seems clear that client deterioration can occur when certain clients are exposed to therapeutic techniques that break down and undermine their coping strategies or defenses. Beutler et al. (1984) found that clients in an acute, short-term group inpatient treatment had a significant degree of deterioration. The expressive-experiential treatment of this group emphasized emotional expression, breaking down defenses, and emotional release. In the NIMH Collaborative Depression study, Ogles, Sawyer, and Lambert (1993) reported that negative effects might be related to the theoretical orientation of the counselor. In this study, clients receiving cognitive-behavioral therapy had a greater chance of a negative outcome. In a somewhat similar finding, Gurman and Kniskern (1978, 1986) found that the likelihood of negative effects went up when individual treatment (vs. conjoint treatment) of marital distress was used. All of these results suggest that preventing deterioration may depend on the skillful application of appropriately chosen treatment techniques.

Are the Major Theoretical Approaches Effective?

Since establishing the robust nature of effectiveness, the majority of outcome research has been devoted to examining the efficacy of various theoretical-based approaches to psychotherapy. Unfortunately, of the over 400 different therapies (Kazdin, 1994), few have been empirically tested. Here we address the research trends supporting the efficacy of experiential, client-centered, cognitive-behavioral, behavioral, and psychodynamic approaches to counseling.

Greenberg, Elliott, and Lietaer (1994) conducted a meta-analysis of studies of experiential therapies (client-centered, nondirective and supportive, emotionally focusing and gestalt, cathartic-emotive). The average effect size for this group of experiential therapists was 1.24. These effect sizes were strongest at posttreatment (ES = 1.51), but remained robust at follow-up (ES = 1.16). Thus, in these tests of experiential therapy, the average client could be expected to move from the 50th to the 90th percentile in relation to his or her pretreatment scores. A subset of these studies compared experiential therapy to clients in wait list or no-treatment control groups. The effect size in this analysis was also significant (ES = 1.30). Thus, the average client in experiential treatments is better off than he or she was before treatment and better off than clients not treated.

One of the recent areas of research activity with experiential therapies has focused on what Greenberg et al. (1994) called "process-experiential therapies." In general, this approach involves a client-centered relationship within which the counselor uses more active interventions, including two-chair work, for resolving conflicts and identifying and clarifying emotions (see Greenberg, Rice, & Elliott, 1993, for a more thorough description of this approach). A number of recent studies have found this approach to be relatively successful with a variety of client problems. Elliott et al. (1990) and Jackson and Elliott (1990) found process-experiential treatment of depressed clients to produce significant client improvement. In investigating the resolution of unfinished emotional issues with significant others, Paivio and Greenberg (1992) found empty-chair dialogue that is conducted within the process-experiential approach more successful than educational interventions.

There is probably no approach more studied than client-centered therapy. A number of recent studies provide continued support for the efficacy of client-centered therapy. For example, of the studies in their meta-analysis, Greenberg et al. (1994) calculated the average effect size of client-centered therapy to be 1.15. These studies have ranged across client-problem types that include generalized anxiety (Borokoveck, 1991), high functioning schizophrenics (Teusch, 1990), clients with varied interpersonal problems (Grawe, Caspar, & Ambuhl, 1990), and agoraphobics (Teusch & Boehme, 1991).

Much of the current study of client-centered therapies is being conducted through two European psychotherapy projects. The Hamburg project has produced a series of studies of client-centered work with clients with psychosomatic disorders (Meyer, 1981; Stuhr & Meyer, 1991). The results indicate that both client-centered therapy and psychodynamic treatment make significant improvements in symptom reduction (e.g., depression) when compared to wait list controls. The two treatments are, however, not significantly different. The Berne Psychotherapy Project (Grawe et al., 1990) conducted a series of studies comparing behavior therapy, client-centered therapy, and interactive behavior therapy. Using a wide spectrum of outcome measures (goal attainment scales, symptom measures, and measures of experiential functioning), they found the three treatments to be effective, but again, no different. Thus, the evidence suggests that client-centered therapy is effective with various types of client problems.

Cognitive and cognitive-behavioral models of psychological treatment have also undergone extensive empirical review. Much of the support for the efficacy of cognitive and cognitive-behavioral approaches comes from studies of the treatment of depression, and more recently, panic attacks. Dobson (1989) reviewed studies involving unipolar depression among clinical outpatients, and concluded that cognitive therapy was more effective than no treatment or nonspecific treatments. Dobson also found that cognitive-behavioral therapy was at least as effective as other psychosocial interventions. Either focused cognitive therapy or cognitive-behavioral approaches, which combine cognitive restructuring of catastrophic cognitions with relaxation, have been found to be most successful in the treatment of panic attacks (Barlow et al., 1989; Beck, Sokol, Clark, Berchick, & Wright, 1992; Sokol, Beck, Greenberg, Wright, & Berchick, 1989) and generalized anxiety disorder (Butler, Fennell, Robson, & Gelder, 1991).

It is difficult to isolate the efficacy of treatments exclusive to behavior therapy. Most behavioral approaches now include a cognitive component. However, behavioral approaches have also garnered a sizable research base. Sloan et al. (1975), in a clinical study of neurotic outpatients, compared dynamic treatments with behavioral therapy. Behavior therapy was successful with a wide range of clients at both posttreatment assessment and follow-up when compared to no-treatment controls. Early meta-analyses also generated some support for behavior therapies. Smith et al. (1980), for example, found that behavioral approaches were more effective than some other approaches with a variety of clients and problems. Other reviews support the general efficacy of behavioral counseling (Dobson, 1989; Robinson et al., 1990; Svartberg & Stiles, 1991).

Like other specific approaches, psychodynamic treatments also seem to be generally effective. Svartberg and Stiles (1991) reviewed studies that examined the effects of short-term dynamic therapy. Their analysis revealed that, with various clients and problems, short-term dynamic therapy was superior to the no-treatment groups at both posttreatment and follow-up assessment. The dynamic treatment was, however, significantly less effective when compared to cognitive-behavioral treatment. Crits-Christoph (1992) investigated studies of short-term dynamic therapy in a meta-analysis of only those studies that used treatment manuals to ensure treatment integrity. Clients in short-term dynamic treatment improved significantly more than those in the no-treatment conditions and wait list groups (ES = .81 to 1.10). There were, however, no differences between the dynamic treatment and the alternative treatments studied. Anderson and Lambert (1995) also reviewed studies of short-term dynamic therapy and in two different meta-analyses found effect sizes ranging from .34 to .71.

A number of clinical trials found results similar to those of meta-analytic reviews. In a well-conducted and controlled clinical trial study comparing psychodynamic and interpersonal treatment with cognitive-behavioral therapy for depression, Shapiro, Barkham, Hardy, and

Morrison (1990) found dynamic treatment effective, but less so than cognitive-behavioral treatments. Piper, Azim, Joyce, and McCallum (1991) investigated the efficacy of short-term dynamic therapy and found successful outcome was related to interventions oriented toward improving the therapeutic alliance, but not to the proportion of interpretation offered by the therapist. Henry, Strupp, Butler, Schacht, and Binder (1993) conducted a 5-year study of time-limited (25 sessions) dynamic psychotherapy. Both Piper et al. (1991) and Henry et al. (1993) reported that as the frequency of therapist interpretations increased, measure of the alliance and outcome decreased. The therapists who used more interpretations were perceived by their clients as impatient, less approving, and authoritarian. In their qualitative review of clinical studies, Henry, Strupp, Schacht, and Gaston (1994) suggested that transference interpretations—a hallmark of dynamic therapy—are not universally effective and may even be countertherapeutic under certain conditions.

In conclusion, each of the major theoretical approaches (experiential, behavioral, cognitive, and cognitive-behavioral) has research evidence to support their efficacy. It is important to remember that the best of these studies use manual-guided treatments. As a result, each study could guarantee that the approach was conducted as it was intended.

Which Theoretical Approach is Best?

The question about which of these approaches is best has spawned a number of comparative outcome studies (Luborsky, Singer, & Luborsky, 1975; Smith et al., 1980). To date, outcome research has been unable to establish that any one of the theoretical schools of counseling is superior to any other (Garfield & Bergin, 1986; Lambert, 1991; Smith et al., 1980). Stiles et al. (1986) concluded that, based on the substantial body of evidence, the different therapeutic approaches are essentially equivalent in the outcomes they produce. Using the words of the dodo bird in *Alice in Wonderland,* Luborsky et al. (1975) proclaimed that "Everyone has won and all must have prizes."

There are, however, some exceptions. Meta-analyses have consistently shown small but consistent advantages for cognitive and behavioral approaches when compared to traditional verbal and relationship-based therapies. These advantages seem to be most apparent with targeted and specific client problems, such as phobic, anxiety, and skill deficit problems (Dush, Hirt, & Schroeder, 1983; Lambert, Shapiro, et al., 1986; Miller & Berman, 1983; Nicholson & Berman, 1983). Closer examination of these claims of superiority has, however, led some to question their reliability. For example, in a recent review of comparative outcomes for depression, Robinson et al. (1990) found cognitive and cognitive-behavioral treatment superior to behavior treatment alone; and cognitive, cognitive-behavioral, and behavioral treatments superior to standard verbal therapies. Remarkably, Robinson et al. (1990) found that when the allegiance of the experimenter was taken into account, the differences between treatments vanished.

The best illustration of a head-to-head test of theoretical approaches comes from two clinical trial studies that are noteworthy for their methodological quality. The recent NIMH Collaborative Depression study (Elkin et al., 1989) compared cognitive-behavioral therapy, interpersonal therapy, and a placebo medication control group (see Chapter 2 for further details of this study). The results suggest that there were no differences between interpersonal therapy and cognitive-behavioral therapy. The Second Sheffield Psychotherapy Project (Shapiro et al., 1990) compared psychodynamic, interpersonal, and cognitive-behavioral therapies for depression. Therapist adherence to treatment protocols was ensured, and the relationship factors that may have been common between the treatments was identical. Of 117 clients in the study, cognitive-behavioral treatment was superior to the psychodynamic-interpersonal treatment. In addition, clients with milder and moderate depression levels improved as much in 8 as they did in 16 sessions at posttreatment and follow-up.

These results have produced an interesting paradox for the practitioner. On the one hand, empirical research suggests that there is no difference between diverse therapeutic approaches. However, the process and content of various psychotherapeutic approaches is dramatically different. Two major explanations have been proposed in an attempt to understand this apparent paradox. One argument asserts that differences among approaches do exist, but they have not been found because of methodology problems (Kazdin, 1986; Stiles et al., 1986). For example, some comparative studies use faulty research designs and imprecise outcome measures (Kazdin, 1986;

Mischel, 1977; Stiles et al., 1986). Other studies have obscured possible theoretical differences by using client samples that are so heterogeneous that any effects are lost in averaging across groups. Other ways that true differences could be concealed is by involving different types of settings (e.g., inpatient and outpatient settings) and by using unmonitored therapists who are not actually providing the prescribed treatment. Similarly, the research concerning differences in theoretical approaches is often disseminated in research reviews, where there also can be methodological problems that obscure theoretical differences. Many qualitative reviews use narrative or box score methods that have been criticized because of their imprecise methods of identifying differences.

The second argument proposes that these seemingly different counseling approaches actually share common processes. It is these common process that account for meaningful change in counseling. These common factors are the topic of the next section. Regardless of the reason, it is important to remember that the question about which approaches are most effective is both theoretically and methodologically complex (Stiles et al., 1986).

Are There Common Factors Shared by all Approaches?

The evidence that has accumulated through our study of counseling outcomes increasingly supports the notion that effective counseling, regardless of its theoretical allegiance, contains common factors that contribute to its curative nature. Support for the importance of common factors is now widely evident. In their qualitative review of outcome studies, Lambert and Bergin (1994) concluded that common factors operating across various treatment modalities account for a substantial amount of the improvement found in outcome investigations (see Table 3.1). For example, the NIMH multisite Collaborative Depression study, which involved head-to-head comparisons of cognitive-behavioral, interpersonal, and drug treatments, found few differences between these approaches. This finding led these researchers to suggest that many of the approaches shared common factors that were effective in treating depression (Elkin et al., 1989).

After a thorough examination of the literature, Lambert (1986) concluded that it is safe to say that factors common across counseling approaches account for a substantial amount of client improvement

Table 3.1 *Common factors across therapies associated with positive outcomes*

Support Factors	Learning Factors	Action Factors
Catharsis	Advice	Behavioral regulation
Identification with therapist	Affective experiencing	Cognitive mastery
Mitigation of isolation	Assimilation of problematic experiences	Encouragement of facing fears
Positive relationship	Changing expectations for personal effectiveness	Taking risks
Reassurance	Cognitive learning	Mastery efforts
Release of tension	Corrective emotional experience	Modeling
Structure	Exploration of internal frame of reference	Practice
Therapeutic alliance	Feedback	Reality testing
Therapist/client active participation	Insight	Success experience
Therapist expertness	Rationale	Working through
Therapist warmth, respect, empathy, acceptance, genuineness		
Trust		

Note. From "The Effectiveness of Psychotherapy," by M. J. Lambert and A. E. Bergin, 1994, In A. E. Bergin and S. L. Garfield (Eds.), *Handbook of Psychotherapy and Behavior Change*, 4th ed., pp. 143–189. Copyright 1994 by John Wiley & Sons. Reprinted with permission.

(Lambert, 1986). Lambert (1991) also argued that if one were to determine the percentage of improvement in clients as a function of different factors, 40% would be due to extratherapeutic change factors, 15% would be due to expectancy or placebo effects, 15% would be attributed to specific psychological techniques, and 30% would be accounted for by common factors evident in all therapies regardless of the therapist's theoretical orientation. If this analysis is correct, the impact of these common factors is twice that of specific psychological techniques.

Common factors might best be organized into three categories (Lambert & Bergin, 1994). *Support factors* include catharsis, positive relationship with the therapist, a therapeutic alliance, and the therapist's warmth, respect, and empathy toward and trust of the client. *Learning factors* include advice, affective experiencing, corrective emotional experiencing, feedback, and assimilation of problematic experience. *Action factors* include behavioral regulation, cognitive mastery, facing fears, mastery efforts, and successful experiences. According to Lambert and Bergin (1994), these factors provide for a cooperative working alliance that leads to successful change. Table 3.1 is a summary of Lambert's common factor model.

Elements of the Therapeutic Process: An Organizing Model

The research findings we have presented in this chapter suggest that counseling is effective, its course is relatively short-term, and its effects are lasting. But, our major theoretical schools, although effective, seem no better than one another. Instead, it seems that there is some set of common elements and process underlying successful therapy. We have developed a process based model of counseling that contains those elements common among the various approaches to counseling. A number of other generic models of counseling process have been developed for similar purposes (Orlinsky et al., 1994; Sexton & Whiston, 1991). The current model incorporates previous paradigms in order to reflect the commonly accepted ingredients in counseling and psychotherapy. We present it here as a framework within which to organize the findings presented in this chapter and as a foundation for the remainder of the chapters in this section. Figure 3.2 is a graphical model of our process-based approach.

Figure 3.2 *Process-based Counseling Model*

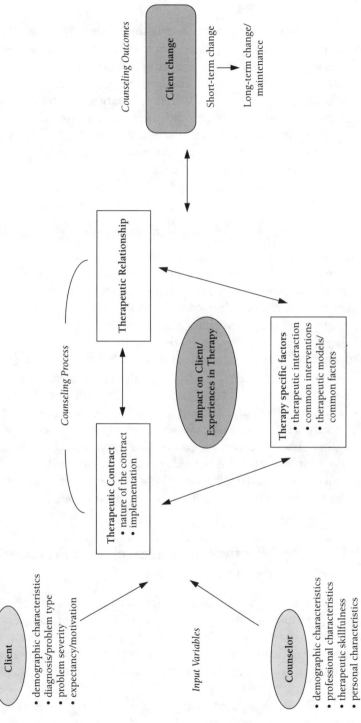

The counseling process and its outcomes are first influenced by various preexisting characteristics that the client and counselor bring with them into the therapeutic process (input variables). Some of these characteristics are stable (demographics, personality style, personal history), whereas others are subject to change during the course of counseling (beliefs, attitudes, expectations).

Once counseling begins, there are at least three primary factors that impact outcome. The therapeutic contract includes structural factors of counseling (fees, duration, role structuring). (For a more detailed discussion of these typical structural elements see Orlinsky et al., 1994.) Both the nature of that contract and the manner in which it is implemented are important. The therapeutic relationship is a central element in all counseling models. From our perspective, the relationship includes the personal connection between client and counselor, the therapeutic alliance that develops, and the nature of the interactional dynamics that characterizes that relationship. Within that relationship specific techniques and interventions are used to promote client change. The specific nature of the techniques depends on the setting; individual counseling techniques are different than those approaches used in schools (see Figure 3.2).

The combination of relationship, structure, and technique results in certain in-session experiences for both the client and counselor. It may be that the client develops insight, gains some measure of awareness, expresses emotional affect, and develops a sense of mastery. The outcomes of counseling vary according to the setting and client, but all have both short- and long-term dimensions. It is important to note that we view these elements of therapeutic process to be reciprocal in their influences on one another.

Integrating Effectiveness Research Into Practice: Conclusions and Implications

The results of clinical trial and meta-analytic studies provide a wide array of empirical findings regarding the efficacy of counseling. Based on the current state of this literature, we can confidently make six major conclusions regarding the effectiveness of counseling; these conclusions have implications for counseling practice and education.

1. The accumulated evidence leads to a relatively clear conclusion: Counseling is a process from which most clients who become

involved with skilled therapists benefit. When compared to effect size changes in other fields, those produced by various methods of psychotherapy are typically as large or larger than those resulting from medical and educational interventions (Lambert & Bergin, 1994). Using Cohen's (1977) method of evaluating effect sizes, the magnitudes in the evaluation of counseling can be considered to be statistically large. Significant positive change is also evident when one calculates the percentage of clients improving. Lambert, Shapiro, et al., (1986) concluded that 65% of all clients will make improvements in counseling. These changes are consistently greater than no-treatment, wait list, and placebo-treatment control groups.

However, not all counseling is helpful. Of the clients seeking our help, studies consistently find that somewhere between 6% and 11% of the clients get worse rather than better. Cause of this deterioration has yet to be clearly identified, but many reports now cite the counselor as the primary influence of negative outcome.

2. Outcome studies have demonstrated the general effectiveness of a number of the major therapeutic approaches. The general conclusion is that all of these approaches seem relatively equal in their effectiveness. An exception to this conclusion is a small advantage found for some approaches (e.g., cognitive, cognitive-behavioral) with certain client problems. Such findings are certainly a paradox for practitioners. Different clinicians describe and act in very different ways with clients. However, from a research perspective their efforts seem to be equal. In part, this is due to the immense complexity of the question of differential effectiveness. Thousands of client, therapist, contextual, treatment, and other factors go into the equation regarding what is "best."

Thus, claims of equality appear to be somewhat premature, given the theoretical and methodological complexities associated with comparative outcome studies. What does seem clear is that simply choosing a school of counseling will not guarantee that a practitioner is effective. Instead, practitioners need to develop complex schemes that integrate information from various sources in making clinical decisions.

3. There are common factors evident across various therapeutic approaches that significantly contribute to successful counseling. If the effects of various influences that contribute to client change are partialed out, approximately 30% of the outcome variance can be

attributed to nonspecific factors that seem evident in all therapies, regardless of the theoretical allegiance. When compared to the 15% attributable to specific therapeutic techniques, these nonspecific factors are significant. Unfortunately, we do not have a clear idea of what factors make up the common elements of therapy. We propose that what is common to successful therapy is a process conducted by a skilled therapist who helps the client get invested and involved in the process, and uses techniques that are matched to the client and based on a therapeutic relationship.

4. The increasing trend toward eclecticism and integration evident among practitioners is supported by the current research evidence. In fact, many have suggested that the era of "theory specific" research and practice may be gone (Bergin & Garfield, 1994). Instead, the focus of attention for both researchers and practitioners are those common elements that contribute to successful counseling. However, as the next chapter will demonstrate, specific techniques have been found to be more effective with certain client problems. The selection of techniques should, then, be individualized and depend on the client rather than on the counselor's adherence to a counseling theory.

The current debate centers around the differences between integrated and eclectic models. Eclectic approaches are characterized by atheoretical, pragmatic collections of divergent techniques that some suggest lacks a systematic model to guide practice (Norcross & Grencavage, 1989). The integration-based approach is based on a higher order set of constructs that account for change and help guide the practitioner in clinical decision making. An advantage of an integrated approach is that as new research is developed, it can be incorporated into an existing conceptual framework. Unfortunately, the development of integrated approaches is only beginning. Orlinsky et al. (1994), Prochaska (1991), and Norcross and Grencavage (1989) are among those developing such models. It may be that even the process-based model presented here can serve as a model by which to understand the important elements in counseling practice.

Many counselor education programs take a theory-based approach to teaching counseling practice. Such an approach places importance on counseling theory as a primary guide for the student counselor to use in understanding what goes on between counselor and clients. The alternative for both education and practice appears to be an integrated approach in which common factors stand at the center.

5. One of the more disturbing results of these outcome data is the number of clients who either do not use or do not continue with counseling. Many of these clients reach an acceptable degree of change and discontinue therapy. The outcome data suggest that a myriad of ethnic, economic, and social factors also contribute to their lack of attendance. In addition, the manner in which we traditionally provide counseling services may limit our ability to serve certain clients. Because there are so many clients who do not use our services, we may need to become more accessible, more affordable, and more flexible in delivering those services.

For clients who do begin counseling, practitioners need to ensure that the client is engaged. The results presented here suggest that the counselor's actions are what are most important in keeping clients in therapy. In addition, we need to begin to consider the client's current stage within the change process in determining how to structure counseling. Prochaska (1991) proposed a stages-of-change model that matches counseling interventions with the client readiness for change. Prochaska suggested that clients drop out of counseling because there is a mismatch between their stage in the change process and the counselor's intervention. For example, clients may be in an early stage of change and the counselor may intervene as if they are ready to initiate specific actions. In research with clients hoping to quit smoking, Prochaska found that of the 40% of clients who typically dropped out, most could be enticed to continue if the interventions were changed so they matched the client's stage within the change process.

6. The optimal duration of counseling is a topic of continuing debate, particularly in light of the economic pressures in the mental health marketplace. In general it seems that the road to recovery via counseling can be considered to be a relatively short one (Lambert & Cattani-Thompson, 1996; Steenbarger, 1994). For the practitioner, these findings, coupled with the economic pressures of mental health services, suggest that the development of short-term approaches to counseling is called for. This is not to say that counseling practitioners should adopt a short-term theory (e.g., solution-focused approaches). Instead, it is a call for us to think of our work as occurring in a relatively short time frame, within which we need to implement those elements of effective counseling. Models like the one developed by Steenbarger (1994) delineate the common elements of such a short-term perspective.

In the next three chapters we build on these general trends by focusing attention on specific areas in which counseling practitioners function—mental health, school, and career counseling. Counselors working in these areas make use of different methods and have different outcome goals. We believe that there are many common research-based findings that apply across these settings. Thus, the suggestions we make regarding individual counseling apply, to some degree, to other settings. Likewise, work with career and school populations has identified trends applicable to individual counseling. To organize these presentations we will continue to rely on the process-based model identified in this chapter (see Figure 3.2).

CHAPTER 4

Factors That Contribute to Effective Individual Counseling

Regardless of one's theoretical allegiance, it seems safe to say that all forms of counseling, to one degree or another, operate according to the general principles that govern effective behavior change. The school counselor uses behavior change principles in those interactions with students that take place during short time periods in the hallway, individually in an office, or during classroom contacts. The career counselor uses these same principles in counseling clients across the life-span, whether individually or within groups, whether in schools or in private centers. For mental health counselors behavior change principles form the foundation for systematically planned therapeutic interventions used to remediate a variety of emotional concerns. We think that the collective body of empirical evidence regarding counseling outcomes has much to offer both practicing counselors and counselor educators in their understanding of the basic principles of counseling.

After several decades of counseling outcome research, most researchers agree that counseling is an enterprise in which clients working with skilled counselors can benefit (see Chapter 3). The purpose of this chapter is to explore and identify those factors that contribute significantly to effective individual counseling. We are interested in two primary questions, What common elements of individual counseling contribute to positive outcomes? and Are there ways to enhance already effective counseling? To answer the first, we investigate the elements of the process-based counseling model presented in Chapter 3 (see Figure 3.2). To answer the second, we look at the research for client-process and counselor matching as a mechanism for furthering the goal of effective behavior change.

What About Individual Counseling is Effective?

The outcome research offers a wealth of information regarding the components of counseling that contribute positively to client change. As you will remember from the last chapter (see Figure 3.2), we see counseling as a process-based model. In the following sections we consider the empirical evidence that helps explain each element in the model. This evidence paints a picture of the important elements in effective individual counseling.

Client and Counselor Characteristics

Considerable effort has been devoted to the study of both clients and counselors. Propelled by Frank's (1971) claim that the client is the single most influential factor in counseling, research efforts have been aimed at identifying profiles of those clients who will benefit most from our services. Similar attention has also been focused on identifying the characteristics of an ideal counselor. Unfortunately, although these research studies produced some useful results, the current consensus among researchers is that identifying an ideal client and counselor is overly simplistic and cannot represent the complex interactions that take place in counseling. Consequently, research focusing on client or therapist characteristics has decreased in recent years (Garfield, 1994; Goldfield, Greenberg, & Marhar, 1990), and interest in the study of interactions among clients, counselors, and treatment modalities has increased (Beutler, Machado, & Neufeldt, 1994).

Which Client Characteristics are Important?

Early research into client factors was commonly based on correlational studies attempting to link certain client demographic characteristics with successful outcomes. Most of these broad demographic characteristics did not prove to be a fruitful focus for research. For example, outcome was not related to social class (Garfield, 1986; Luborsky, Chandler, Auerbach, Cohen, & Bachrach, 1971); racial match (Jones, 1982), age (Frank, Kupfer, & Perel, 1989; Rounsaville, Weissear, & Prusoff, 1981), gender (Jones & Zoppel, 1982), or initial client motivation (Horowitz, Marmar, Weiss, DeWitt, & Rosenbaum, 1984).

One client demographic consistently related to outcome is the level of disturbance. In general, the more disturbed the client, the lower the potential outcome (Stone, Green, Gleser, Whitman, & Roster, 1975). In a major qualitative review, Orlinsky et al. (1994) suggested that patient suitability for treatment (including client diagnosis) was a significant variable in studies spanning the last 40 years. The influence of client diagnosis is most apparent in the study of depression, where those clients who are most depressed remain most depressed even after psychotherapy (Burns & Nolen-Hoeksema, 1991; Steinmetz, Lewinsohn, & Antonuccio, 1983). This trend, however, is not as evident in other clinical populations where the symptom profiles are less stable.

Historically, there has also been great interest in understanding the role of client expectancy. Frank (1959) was among the first to suggest that expectancy and outcome were linked. Early studies were consistent with Frank's claims—the greater the expectancy the better the outcome (Friedman, 1963; Goldstein, 1960). However, recent reviews report that pretreatment expectation levels are not necessarily related to outcome (Garfield, 1994). To date, no definitive conclusions can be reached regarding the role of client expectation.

These equivocal findings concerning client expectations are somewhat perplexing. One explanation is that studies of expectations suffer from methodological problems that contribute to the mixed results. For example, various operational definitions of expectancy are used across studies. Mathews, Johnston, Shaw, and Gelder (1974) operationalized expectations in a way that conceptually resembles Bandura's (1986) construct of self-efficacy; others defined expectancy as a belief in the techniques or as confidence in the therapist. A second explanation is that the point at which expectations are measured is critical but has yet to be incorporated into research studies. Some studies have found the level of expectation in the early phases of counseling to be better predictors of outcome than expectation levels before treatment commences (Mathews et al., 1976; Tollinton, 1973).

In a review of studies of expectancy of systematic desensitization, Perotti and Hopewell (1980) differentiated two kinds of expectancy—initial and developed. Initial expectancies are those beliefs that the client brings to treatment, and developed expectancies are a function of progress within counseling. It may be that initial expectancies function more to help clients become involved in counseling rather than to have a direct impact on the final outcome (Thurer & Hursh, 1981). Future research should follow the lead of Perotti and Hopewell (1980) and more precisely define the types of expectancy.

What Counselor Characteristics are Important?

There is a historically rooted belief that personal characteristics of the counselor are the essential ingredients in successful counseling (Rogers, 1957). Early studies (particularly in the 1960s and 1970s) attempted to identify these personal characteristics but, like similar studies of clients, found that simple correlational investigations provided few concrete answers. More recent studies have focused less on personal and more on objective and therapeutic-related characteristics (e.g., skillfulness, relational style, and cognitive complexity). The studies in these areas have provided more fruitful results.

There seems to be sufficient evidence to suggest that there are some counselor characteristics that are critical components in the outcome puzzle. Studies of general counseling effectiveness consistently find that the degree of benefit is more highly related to the therapist than to any particular technique or therapeutic modality (Crits-Christoph & Mintz, 1991; Lambert, 1989; Luborsky et al., 1986). These same studies show that some counselors produce consistently more positive results than do others (Lafferty, Beutler, & Crago, 1989; Lambert, 1989). The particular contribution of counselors can be summarized by research in four areas: demographic (age, sex, ethnicity), professional characteristics (experience, training, discipline), therapeutic skill (therapeutic orientation, skillfulness), and personal characteristics (relational style, personality type, emotional well-being).

Demographic characteristics. The effort to identify significant demographic characteristics has contributed little to clarifying what counselor factors are related to successful counseling. For example, studies of both counselor age and sex are mixed—some found no variation in outcome due to age alone (Atkinson & Schein, 1986; Beck, 1988), others reported age similarity to be important (Beck, 1988), and still others concluded that younger therapists can successfully treat older clients (Thompson & Gallagher, 1984; Thompson, Gallagher, & Breckenridge, 1987).

One problem is that there are few methodologically sound studies investigating the influence of the counselors' gender. Beutler, Crago, and Arizmendi (1986) did find preliminary support for the possibility that female therapists may have better results with female clients. In a clinical trial study, Jones, Krupnick, and Kerig (1987) investigated both outcome and satisfaction indices of female clients treated by both male and female therapists. They controlled for therapist training and experience, used manualized treatment protocols, randomly assigned clients, and ensured equivalency of the severity of the client problem. At both posttherapy and follow-up, there was significant symptom improvement for those clients whose therapists were female. Unfortunately, the absence of male clients in this study makes it difficult to confirm the preliminary findings of Beutler et al. (1986) and test the therapist-client sex match.

Ethnicity has also been a topic of considerable study. Most of these studies focused on ethnic similarity between counselors and clients. Three reviews (Atkinson, 1985; Atkinson & Schein, 1986; Whiston & Sexton, 1993) all reported equivocal results regarding the importance of ethnic similarity regarding counseling outcome. One typical difference between studies is that they use diverse operational definitions of outcome and the nature of the findings seems to depend on those definitions. For example, Atkinson (1985) found that African American clients preferred to work with ethnically similar therapists but this preference was not evident for other ethnic groups. Beck (1988) found that Hispanic clients were more satisfied with counseling when their counselor was Hispanic but this was not the case for African American clients. However, in both of these studies, there was no relationship between outcome and ethnic similarity. In a large-scale naturalistic study of 164 African American and 136 ethnically diverse therapists regarding satisfaction with counseling and symptom reduction, Jones (1982) concluded that neither the ethnicity of the counselor nor the ethnic similarity had any significant impact on the outcome measures. If you measure outcome by the drop-out rate, then ethnic similarity does seem to be important. White counselors working with ethnic minorities have more clients drop out (Atkinson & Schein, 1986; Terrell & Terrell, 1984). Consequently, conclusions regarding the role of ethnicity need to be based on future studies where these different outcome variables are carefully classified.

Professional characteristics. Counselor training programs, state licensing requirements, and national certification criteria are all based on the premise that professionally trained counselors are more effective than those without training. The topics that have had substantial study and provide stable trends for practice are the impact of professional discipline, counselor experience, and professional training.

On a global level, there seems to be little difference in outcome based on professional discipline. Results from meta-analyses range from moderate support for the differential efficacy of psychologists (Smith et al., 1980) to negligible effects across disciplines (Prioleau, Murdock, & Brody, 1983). In the recent Consumer Reports Survey (Consumer Reports, 1995), volunteer respondents rated psychologists and social workers as being more effective than marriage and family therapists. Seligman (1995) suggested that these differences, although statistically significant, were more a reflection of the nature of the problems encountered by these different groups rather than a reflection of skill.

There is curiously little empirical support for the time and energy invested in professionally preparing counselors. Some qualitative reviews concluded that there is no relationship between outcomes and either training or experience (Auerbach & Johnson, 1977; Beutler et al., 1986; Christenson & Jacobson, 1993), whereas others have suggested that experienced therapists have better outcomes than those with less experience (Baekeland & Lundwall, 1975; Lyons & Woods, 1991). Meta-analytic reviews also report mixed findings. Both Berman and Norton (1985) and Weisz, Weiss, Alicke, and Klotz (1987) found that professionally trained counselors had no systematic advantage over nonprofessional therapists. In a meta-analysis exclusively of short-term analytic therapy, Crits-Christoph et al. (1991) found the experience level of the therapist to be significantly and positively related to counseling outcome. The most recent meta-analysis investigated both experience and training (Stein & Lambert, 1995). They found no relationship between outcome and experience, but found improved success rates for those counselors who were professionally trained.

If we are going to understand the impact of counselor experience and training, we need to move toward realistic investigations that consider characteristics of the client, the therapeutic modality, and the context of therapy (Beutler et al., 1994). There is already some evidence to support this position. For example, close examination of the two reviews cited above reveals a somewhat different picture when the experience-modality interaction is considered. In the Berman and Norton (1985) study, professionally trained counselors using short-term treatments were more effective with older clients than those who were not trained. In the Weisz et al. (1987) study, professionally trained therapists, when compared to their untrained counterparts, had superior outcomes with younger clients who over-controlled their feelings. Stein and Lambert (1995) found that therapist experience became more important as the severity of the client disturbance increased—more experienced therapists were more effective at producing and retaining successful outcomes with the more severely disturbed clients. Curiously, in their meta-analysis, Svartberg and Stiles (1991) found therapeutic efficacy decreased with experience!

Most of the studies investigating counselor experience presuppose that practitioners with similar experience levels have the same skill levels. As Beutler et al. (1994) suggested, exposure to training and practice does not necessarily result in skill acquisition. In fact, Shaw and Dobson (1988) argued that practice, supervision, and experience of therapy behaviors are not necessarily related to therapeutic skill. Thus, the therapist's professional contribution to outcome is better measured when based on an evaluation of the counselor's demonstrated skill.

Therapeutic skill. It is remarkable that so few attempts have been made to empirically determine the relationship between therapist skill and outcome. In a review of 359 outcome studies, Moncher and Prinz (1991) concluded that most studies either ignored or failed to adequately control for therapist competence and skill. When it is considered, counselor skill makes an important contribution to successful outcome. Orlinsky et al. (1994) found therapist skill to be among the most salient variables that contribute to successful therapeutic outcome. Of the studies reviewed, 68% found that various measures of therapist skill had a significantly positive impact on outcome (ES = .20). Similarly, Bennun and Schindler (1988) found therapist competence and skill contributed to the ability of the counselor to create facilitative conditions and positive outcome. In addition, Crits-Christoph, Cooper, and Luborsky (1988) found high levels of counselor skill to be significantly related to successful counseling.

The introduction of treatment manuals into outcome research has enhanced the study of therapist skillfulness. Manuals standardize psychotherapeutic interventions by specifically outlining the details of a particular type of intervention. Crits-Christoph et al. (1991) found that treatment manuals reduced the variability in outcome results attributable to the counselor. A significant positive relationship between the degree to which the therapist complied with the manual and positive outcome were demonstrated by both Luborsky et al. (1985) and Shaw (1983). However, Henry et al. (1993) found that although technical proficiency increased with manualized treatment, relationship skill and supportiveness declined. In their meta-analysis of depression treatment, Robinson et al. (1990) found equivalent effect sizes for studies that incorporated treatment manuals and studies that did not. However, at a 1-year follow-up, clients treated by counselors trained with treatment manuals experienced fewer symptoms and problems than those clients treated by therapists not using manuals.

Above and beyond technical skill there is something about therapeutic styles that influences outcome. A number of naturalistic studies investigated, for example, therapist directiveness. *Directiveness* is a therapist's active involvement in determining the direction, necessary events, and intervention that needs to take place in counseling. Each of these studies found a somewhat positive relationship between therapist directiveness and outcome (Elliot, Baker, Caskey, & Pistrange, 1982; Luborsky et al., 1980; McLellan, Woody, Luborsky, & Goehl, 1988). Meta-analytic reviews present another side of the picture. In a study of short-term dynamic therapy, Svartberg and Stiles (1991) found that as the level of therapist directiveness went up, outcome levels decreased. Similarly, Lafferty et al. (1989) found therapist directiveness to be negatively related to symptom reduction.

There is some evidence to suggest that therapist directiveness might be useful with certain types of clients. Beutler, Mohr, Grawe, Engle, and MacDonald (1991) conducted a well-controlled study of the treatment of depression using a manual-based treatment protocol and random assignment to treatment groups. They found that therapists using two different types of treatment with the same level of directiveness were more successful than therapists using nondirective treatments with clients that had been classified as resistance-prone. Conversely, nondirective treatments were more effective with nonresistant clients when compared to directive treatments.

Personal characteristics. Some of our major theoretical models propose that certain personal characteristics of the counselor are essential to successful counseling (e.g., Rogers, 1957). Sorting through the myriad of potentially important personality characteristics is an overwhelming task. Consequently, research in this area has been characterized by a shotgun type approach in which no systematic model of inquiry has been followed. Two particular areas—therapist emotional health and cognitive complexity—have produced promising systematic research.

Many reviews found the adjustment and self-confidence levels of the therapist to be related to outcome (Beutler et al., 1986; Lambert & Bergin, 1983; Sexton & Whiston, 1991). The results, however, are not consistent. Both Antonuccio, Davis, Lewinsohn, and Beckenridge (1982) and Lafferty et al. (1989) found a measure of neuroticism unrelated to therapeutic outcome. In addition, Luborsky et al. (1980) used a theory-specific measure of self-actualization (discrepancy between perceived and ideal self-concepts) and found no significant relationship between therapist actualization and outcome.

A corollary belief is that therapists getting personal therapy may learn more about themselves, become more adjusted and, thus, be more effective. Many counselor training programs require personal therapy or focus considerable attention on personal growth as a means to develop skilled counselors. There is little evidence to suggest there is a relationship between getting therapy and increased efficacy, particularly in comparison with other factors with strong research support (Beutler et al., 1994). Two reviews found inconclusive evidence (Clark, 1986; Greenberg & Stalker, 1981), and two others suggested that in the short run, personal therapy for the therapist may actually inhibit efficacy (Buckley, Karasu, & Charles, 1981; Garfield & Bergin, 1971). Beutler et al. (1994) suggested that this confusing picture might become clearer if we investigated not just whether a therapist received therapy but the reason for that choice as well.

How therapist adjustment fits into the outcome puzzle is difficult to ascertain. Indications are that it is only when the counselor is seriously impaired that counseling is effected. Therefore, it may be that emotional adjustment is a continuous variable, where the degree to which someone is maladjusted is the pertinent factor. If this is the case, one wouldn't expect the mental health of the counselor to impact counseling outcome until he or she was "impaired." The implication is that it would be more efficient to spend time identifying those with significant impairments rather than investing a good deal of energy in improving the emotional health of those who are already relatively well adjusted.

A second personal characteristic with significant research is that of cognitive styles or cognitive complexity. Two studies best illustrate this work. Holloway and Wampold (1986) conducted a meta-analysis on counselor conceptual level. The majority of the studies were analog types using nonclinical clients. The findings have some interesting implications regarding therapist characteristics. They found that counselors, with more conceptually abstract and complex process styles were better able to perform counseling tasks than those with more concrete and nonabstract process styles. In a study of clinical populations, Hunt, Carr, Dagadakis, and Walker (1985) found cognitive style similarity was predictive of premature therapy termination. In addition, after 12 weeks, client-therapist dyads marked by similar cognitive styles produced more symptom changes by the clients. However, after 24 weeks, those differences disappeared.

The Counseling Process

For the purpose of this overview, we have characterized the counseling process as composed of three major elements: the therapeutic contract, the therapeutic relationship, and specific therapy factors. These elements are described in Chapter 3 and are based on our process model of counseling (see Figure 3.2).

Is the therapeutic contract important? The therapeutic contract includes those aspects of counseling that are involved in structuring the session—the setting, format, frequency, and duration of counseling (Beutler & Clarkin, 1990). The contract needs to be viewed both in terms of its contents and the manner in which it is implemented. We do know that even before a contract is established, we can make decisions that impact the eventual outcome of counseling. We have included these aspects here because they represent the broad structure within which counseling is done. For example, we know that it is important to begin counseling as soon as possible after a referral is made. We found that a long wait between applying for and beginning counseling is negatively related to outcome (Luborsky et al., 1988). We also know that clients who missed one of their first four scheduled sessions were significantly more likely to have negative outcomes as compared to those who kept their initial appointments.

One important element of a contract are the structural parameters within which counseling will take place. These are usually either determined or recommended by the counselor. Sometimes the setting in which they work dictates them. There are no consistent findings linking many of the common structural elements of the therapeutic contract with outcome. For example, outcome has not been found to be related to the format (individual vs. group; Neimeyer, Robinson, Berman, & Haykal, 1989); the frequency of therapy (Calvert, Beutler, & Crago, 1988; Orlinsky et al., 1994); whether it is open-ended or time-limited; or whether a fee is charged (Orlinsky et al., 1994).

The manner in which these contractual elements are implemented and the way in which counseling is terminated are important. For example, a collaborative contract in which client and counselor agree on goals and have clear expectations seems to be significantly related to successful outcome (Goldstein, Cohen, Lewis, & Struening, 1988; Orlinsky et al., 1994; Safran & Wallner, 1991; Tracey, 1988). Systematic and mutually agreed on termination is also characteristic of successful counseling (Clemental-Jones, Malan, & Trauer, 1990; Persons, Burns, & Peroff, 1988). Unsuccessful cases were characterized by little discussion of termination, less time spent reviewing the client's counseling experience, less activity to gain closure, and fewer discussions of the client's affective reaction to termination (Quintana & Holahan, 1992). Therefore, a planned termination in which change is attributed to the client contributes to successful outcome.

How important is the counseling relationship? Research has confirmed the experience of many practitioners—the success of any therapeutic endeavor depends on the participants establishing an open, trusting, collaborative relationship (Frank & Gunderson, 1990; Orlinsky & Howard, 1986). Of all the techniques, client-counselor characteristics, and procedures studied, it is only the counseling relationship that is consistently found to contribute to successful counseling (Luborsky et al., 1988; Orlinsky & Howard, 1986; Sexton & Whiston, 1994). Furthermore, failure to form a quality relationship in therapy is associated with client noncompliance (Eisenthal, Emery, Lazare, & Udin, 1979), premature termination (Tracey, 1977), as well as poor outcome (Alexander & Luborsky, 1986).

Unfortunately, determining what is therapeutic about the relationship is more difficult than one might initially imagine. Empirical and theoretical advances in understanding the relationship are often bogged down by narrow and inadequate definitions (Highlen & Hill, 1984). For example, the relationship has, for many counselors, become synonymous with Rogers' (1957) necessary and sufficient counselor-offered conditions (empathy, unconditional positive regard, genuineness, congruence). In fact, many training texts highlight the core conditions as the very definition of what is therapeutic about a counseling relationship. A number of early reviews found support for the therapeutic effectiveness of these conditions (Gurman, 1977; Mitchell, Bozarth, & Kraft, 1977), but recent comprehensive reviews have not found these conditions to be as important as other aspects of the relationship (Beutler et al., 1986; Sexton & Whiston, 1994).

In a systematic review of the counseling relationship literature, Sexton and Whiston (1994) suggested that the nature of the relationship can only be explained when a multidimensional perspective is adopted. Along this line, the outcome research has investigated a number of common relational components.

Therapist empathy. The initial research was based on Rogers' (1957) model of empathy as a necessary and sufficient condition of therapy. Although early research demonstrated a significant relationship between counselor empathy and outcome, recent evidence has challenged these conclusions (Bergin & Suinn, 1975; Lambert & Bergin, 1994). To understand the current research on empathy and counseling outcome, one must look at how empathy is defined. Defined as a coun-selor-offered condition, empathy is not related to outcome. What does seem important is that clients perceive their counselor to be empathetic (Barrett-Lennard, 1962; Martin & Sterne, 1976). Thus, although a counselor may exhibit those characteristics generally defined as empa-thetic, the client may not perceive them as such, and the counselor's empathetic behaviors will have little impact.

We have learned some of the things that contribute to empathy. For example, we know that using analogies (Suit & Paradise, 1985), infrequently offering general advice (Barkham & Shapiro, 1986), and engaging in less self-disclosure (Peca-Baker & Friedlander, 1989) further contribute to being perceived as empathetic by clients. We have also discovered that both counselor gender (females may be ini-tially viewed as more empathetic) and cognitive complexity (the ability to complexly understand the client's perspective) are related to counselors' ability to appear empathetic (Duan & Hill, 1996). Finally, the research literature supports a multistage view of empathy, in which affective and cognitive components are applied in appropri-ate therapeutic situations. The therapeutic impact of empathy proba-bly depends on the particular client, the nature of the relationship, and stage of the counseling process (Duan & Hill, 1996).

Counselor self-disclosure. The therapeutic value of counselor self-disclosure has also been difficult to establish. Research efforts have been met with mixed and often contradictory empirical findings (Sexton & Whiston, 1994). Some researchers found that counselor self-disclosures strengthen client involvement and enhance the posi-tive perception of the counselor (VandeCreek & Angstadet, 1985), whereas others were unable to find such relationships (Cherbosque, 1987; Mallinckrodt & Helms, 1986). In the most extensive review of the research literature, Orlinsky et al. (1994) found only two studies in the last 10 years reporting a significantly positive relationship between therapist disclosure and outcome. They concluded that therapist self-disclosure was rarely associated with counseling out-comes, and when it was, the influence could just as likely be negative rather than positive.

These mixed results can be better explained by taking a more complex look at self-disclosure. In a review of studies involving ther-apy-like situations, Watkins (1990) suggested that self-disclosing statements should be differentiated between those that are self-involving (those statements related to current counseling events) and self-disclosing responses (statements related to something in the counselor's past). Watkins concluded that, in general, self-involving statements were more effective than other types of counselor disclosures. These self-involving counselor responses also have been found to promote higher ratings of counselor social influence (Watkins, Savickas, Brizzi, & Manus, 1990; Watkins & Schneider, 1989).

Counselor congruence. The importance of counselor congruence or genuineness has been theoretically valued (Rogers, 1957), but has not been empirically supported. In and of itself, a congruent presentation by a counselor is not necessarily important (Lambert, Shapiro, et al., 1986). Orlinsky et al. (1994) found that only 38% of the findings supported the relationship between genuineness and outcome. It may be that therapist genuineness and congruence indirectly impact outcome. An incongruent counselor might be perceived by their clients as less involved and less invested in the relationship. However, to date, empirical support for valuing counselor congruence as a crucial therapeutic element is not well documented.

Personal role engagement and investment. Engagement and investment in counseling are critical elements of successful counseling (Allen, Deering, Buskirk, & Coyne, 1988; Saunders, Howard, & Orlinsky, 1989; Sexton & Whiston, 1994). From the client's perspective, believing that one's counselor is relationally involved and invested in the relationship seems particularly important (Jones, Wynne, & Watson, 1986; Orlinsky et al., 1994). An indirect measure of engagement and investment might be the level of client in-session motivation. Orlinsky et al. found that over 50% of studies support the importance of client in-session motivation in general. This is particularly telling given that client motivation measured prior to therapy is not significantly related to successful outcome.

Mutual affirmation. The affiliative nature of the relationship (therapist affirmation, acceptance, positive regard) has been the focus of a number of outcome studies. Although the research supports the importance of these therapist characteristics, the reported effect sizes vary widely (Orlinsky et al., 1994). Thus, it is probably the case that these characteristics may be differentially important, depending on some other aspect of counseling (e.g., the stage, modality, client diagnosis). Less often studied, but equally important, is the affirmation of the counselor by the client (Bachelor, 1991; Quintina & Meara, 1990). According to Orlinsky et al. (1994), affirmation of the counselor by the client may be even more important than the reverse. Regardless of the differential importance, reciprocal affirmation is a crucial aspect of the therapeutic bond (Grawe et al., 1990; Henry, 1990; Sexton & Whiston, 1994).

Collaborative interaction. A sizable number of findings suggest that the therapeutic nature of the relationship is enhanced by collaborative interactions between client and counselor. Counselors who establish collaborative relationships were significantly more successful when compared to those using more directive styles (Bachelor, 1991; Lafferty et al., 1989). Similarly, collaborative clients were usually more successful than those classified as dependent or controlling (Bachelor, 1991; Orlinsky et al., 1994). In an interesting study of collaborative style and the stage of counseling with phobic clients, Schulte and Kunzel (1991) found a positive relationship between outcome and the opportunity for clients to make contributions to therapy in the later stages of the process. This positive relationship between client contribution and outcome was interestingly not evident in the early stages of counseling.

The openness with which the client participates in the counseling interactions is another measure of collaboration. Numerous studies report a positive relationship between client openness and outcome and a negative relationship between client defensiveness and outcome (Grawe, 1989; Henry, 1990). Orlinsky et al. (1994) found that 80% of identified findings support the importance of the client's open (vs. defensive) involvement with the therapist. Schindler (1991) suggested that the effect of client defensiveness depends on the stage of the counseling relationship. In their study, client defensiveness was significantly related to lower outcomes in later, but not earlier, sessions. These results suggest that openness is a relational stance that can be developed in counseling. Thus, initial client defensiveness is not necessarily an indication of poor prognosis. Instead, it seems that enhancing openness may be an important early goal of therapy.

The study of these important elements of the relationship, along with the growing interest in its reciprocal and interactive nature, has spawned three theoretical models that hold great promise in further explaining the therapeutic nature of the counseling relationship.

Models of the Counseling Relationship

The working alliance, social influence, and interactional models of the counseling relationship have received considerable research attention and garnered strong empirical support. The strength of the evidence for these models far exceeds that demonstrated by the prevalent Rogerian model.

Research on the working alliance model (client-counselor agreement on goals, agreement on therapeutic tasks, and the emotional bond between client and counselor) found that successful and unsuccessful cases could be differentiated on the basis of the strength of the working alliance in the first quarter of treatment. In addition, the strength of the working alliance could predict up to 45% of the variance in treatment outcome (Horvath & Greenberg, 1986; Horvath & Symonds, 1991; Luborsky et al., 1988; Morgan, Luborsky, Crits-Christoph, Curtis, & Soloman, 1982). This model directed counselors to broaden their view of the relationship to include task and goal agreement in conjunction with the traditionally accepted emotional side of the relationship

A second perspective that has also garnered strong empirical support is the social influence model (Heppner & Claiborn, 1989). According to the social influence model, the counseling relationship is an interaction between client and counseling, in which the counselor develops a position of influential power by enhancing his or her characteristics of expertness, attractiveness, and trustworthiness, thus becoming a credible and useful resource to the client (Strong, 1968). LaCrosse (1980) found that perceived expertness, attractiveness, and trustworthiness at the completion of counseling accounted for 35% of the variance in outcome as measured by a goal attainment scaling procedure. Therefore, counselors need to consider how they can be perceived by clients as expertlike, attractive, and trustworthy helpers.

The interpersonal complementarity model of the counseling relationship posits that relationships are marked by interpersonal complementary responses in which the interpersonal behavior of the participants endorses and confirms each other's self-presentation. The complementarity of styles will be further examined in research related to enhancing outcomes later in this chapter. In regard to the relationship, current research suggests complementarity to be related to both successful outcome as well as a decrease in dropout rates. In a series of studies, Tracey (1985, 1986) found that there were significantly different patterns of complementarity between successful and unsuccessful counseling dyads. Those that were rated as most successful were composed of counselors who were more dominant (less dependent on the client response for their behavior), whereas unsuccessful dyads displayed equal levels of dominance and control. Interestingly, these differences depended on the stage of counseling. In successful cases, complementarity between the client and counselor is higher in the initial and last stages of counseling, and low in the middle stages. In the initial and middle stages, complementarity was the basis of collaboration and change, respectively, whereas in the later stage it was the foundation of successful termination (Tracey, 1987). The implication is that counselors need to change their relational stance with clients as counseling progresses through the different stages.

Important Therapy-Specific Factors in Successful Counseling

Outside what is generally considered the therapeutic relationship there are therapy-specific factors that contribute to counseling outcome (see Figure 3.2). We see these as distinct from the contract and the relationship. Two such areas have received the most research attention—the focus of the client-counselor conversation and the specific techniques and interventions used.

It seems important that the therapeutic conversation is focused on the clients' specific life problems (Jones, Parke, & Pulos, 1992) or on relationships that are central to these concerns (Jones, Cummings, & Horowitz, 1988). A common belief is that client affect should be a central focus of counseling. The research suggests that focusing on client affect is generally important, but under certain situations may be only somewhat helpful and at other times may be contraindicated (Braswell, Kendall, Braith, Carey, & Vye, 1985; Orlinisky et al., 1994). For example, Beutler et al. (1984) found that inpatients with higher levels of pretreatment distress got significantly worse with affectively focused treatments. The negative outcomes associated with a here and now affective focus may stimulate negative attributions in clients and thus, have an unintended effect (Henry, Schacht, & Strupp, 1990). Sometimes counselors will select a here and now focus to confront the lack of progress. Piper et al. (1991) have found that using those techniques at such times may be more harmful than helpful.

It is not a surprise that many specific therapeutic interventions have been studied. What is surprising is that few of those common techniques are associated with positive outcome and even fewer have strong empirical support. Furthermore, even with those techniques that are directly related to outcome, the impact often depends on some mediating variable (e.g., client distress level, therapist skillfulness, stage). What follows is a brief review of the common techniques that have received the most attention by the empirical research.

Experiential confrontation, for example, was found to be a successful technique in a number of the studies reviewed by Orlinsky et al. (1994). Its use, however, may be contraindicated with certain types of clients. Jones et al. (1988) found that clients with low levels of disturbances (as opposed to those with high disturbance levels) had positive outcomes when the therapist emphasized feelings. Beutler et al. (1984) found participation in an experiential-expressive group treatment approach during psychiatric hospitalization to be associated with negative outcomes. The effectiveness of therapist interpretation is mediated by the type of interpretation and the client disturbance level (Orlinsky et al., 1994). Coady (1991) reported that poorer outcomes were associated with therapist interpretations that did not focus on the therapeutic relationship when compared with interpretations that did focus on the relationship. Jones et al. (1988) found that less disturbed clients benefited from transference interpretations. In two meta-analyses, paradoxical intention was found to be significantly related to outcome (Hill, 1987; Shoran-Salmon & Rosenthal, 1989). When compared to other techniques, however, paradox may be only equally effective (Sexton, Montgomery, Goff, & Nugent, 1993).

A number of commonly accepted therapeutic techniques are less effective than we may believe. Facilitating client exploration (when not specifically problem focused) is minimally effective (Bachelor, 1991; Coady, 1991; Hill et al., 1988), and counselor reflection and clarification are not associated with successful outcome (Coady, 1991; McCullough et al., 1991). In general, advice is more likely to not be helpful (Coady, 1991; Orlinsky et al., 1994), and counselor support and encouragement (as a therapeutic intervention) was important only about one-third of the time (Orlinsky et al., 1994). As one might expect, the contribution of these techniques depends on certain characteristics of the client or the stage of counseling. For example, regarding experiential confrontation, clients with high levels of pretreatment disturbance seem to benefit from direct advice as compared with uncovering and awareness-oriented techniques (Jones et al., 1988). Finally, counselor support was most effective during early but not middle or later sessions (Schindler, 1991).

How can we Further Enhance Good Counseling?

What we have learned from this research is that there is probably no single counselor or client characteristic, no single theory, or no technique that can account for the success of good counseling. In fact, the meta-analytic investigations of therapeutic efficacy show that we actually account for very little of what goes on. What we now know is that successful counseling can be enhanced through careful matching of clients to both counselors and process elements. Most of the research in this area examined the effects of matching in the areas of client-counselor similarity, client-process matching, relational congruence, and client-treatment matching.

Client-Counselor Similarity

Many of the early research efforts in matching focused on client–therapist similarity. In an early review of the similarity concept, Berzins (1977) suggested that although the idea of matching clients and therapists on the basis of attitudes, beliefs, and personal characteristics is appealing, there is little support for the notion. Recent investigations have focused on the impact of client-counselor value and attitude similarity. Attitude similarity has been found to predict client involvement, retention, and positive outcome, and accounts for significantly more outcome variance than demographic similarity (Beutler et al., 1986). A number of qualitative reviews have found that clients tend to adopt the values of the counselors over the course of therapy (Atkinson & Schein, 1986; Beutler & Bergin, 1991; Clarkin, Glick, Haas, & Spencer, 1991; Kelly, 1990).

The best experimental evidence of the influence of client-counselor similarity comes from two studies by Propst (1980) and Propst, Ostrom, Watkins, Dean, and Mashburn (1992), which investigated religious clients and therapists. In the first of these studies, Propst (1980) used a manual-based treatment in which counselor behaviors were self-monitored. She found that religious clients had more symptomatic change when engaged in religiously oriented therapy than those in nonreligious oriented treatments. In the second study, religiously congruent cognitive therapy conducted by nonreligious counselors was more effective than religiously oriented cognitive therapy conducted by religious counselors. These studies suggest that it may not be the actual similarity of client-therapist values, but the therapists' ability to work within and communicate within the client's value system that is most important (Propost, 1980; Propost et al., 1992). Beutler and Clarkin (1990) argued that philosophical similarity may serve to enhance therapeutic engagement, whereas dissimilarity in regard to social attachment and intimacy attitudes may actually enhance therapeutic change.

Client-Process Matching

Some clients seem to respond to different therapeutic modalities more positively than to others. Beutler et al. (1991) investigated outcomes of depressed clients with different coping styles and reactance potentials when receiving three different types of therapy (cognitive, experiential, supportive self-directed therapy). Those clients characterized by an externalizing coping style improved more in cognitive therapy, whereas those classified as nonexternalizing improved most in supportive, self-directed therapy. Resistant clients improved more from self-directed therapy than in the other types of therapy, and low-resistance patients improved more in cognitive therapy than in the self-directed modality. This work is important in that it characterizes clients as to their relational styles and considers the interaction between this style and types of therapeutic interventions, rather than relying on broad, sometimes undefinable, personality variables.

Client Problem-Treatment Matching

The majority of the effort in the area of client-problem treatment matching has gone into the study of those disorders that can be specified (e.g., depression, generalized anxiety disorder, obsessive compulsive disorder, posttraumatic stress disorder, phobias, panic disorders, agoraphobia). With each disorder, a number of important practice implications have emerged.

Depression. Considerable evidence indicates that a variety of cognitive, cognitive-behavioral, and behavioral treatments are successful interventions for depressive disorders (Emmelkamp, 1994). In a recent meta-analysis of depressed outpatient clients, Dobson (1989) concluded that cognitive therapy was more effective than either no-treatment or nonspecific treatments, and equally as effective as alternative psychosocial or drug interventions (Bowers, 1990; Miller, Norman, Keitner, Bishop, & Dow, 1989; Thase, Bowler, & Harden, 1991). Moreover, those clients treated with cognitive therapy were half as likely to relapse or seek additional treatment as clients receiving pharmacotherapy alone (Hollon, Shelton, & Loosen, 1991). There is some evidence that behavioral marital therapy is the treatment of choice when the depressed client is married (O'Leary & Beach, 1990; Jacobson, Dobson, Fluzetti, Schmaling, & Salusky, 1991). Unfortunately, it is currently difficult to specifically determine what about these broad treatments contributes to their success. Although these procedures seem at least as effective as drug therapy in treating depressions, definitive conclusions regarding which treatment is best are still premature (Holon et al., 1991; McLean & Hakstain, 1990; McLean & Taylor, 1992; Miller et al., 1989).

Generalized anxiety. A variety of anxiety management techniques seem most useful for generalized anxiety disorder (Barlow, O'Brien, & Last, 1984). Butler et al. (1991) found that cognitive therapy was more helpful in the treatment of generalized anxiety than no treatment. Comprehensive cognitive therapy packages (such as that of Beck & Emery, 1985) that emphasize insight into irrational beliefs are more effective than diazepam or a placebo (Power, Simpson, Swanson, & Wallace, 1990), equally as effective as anxiety management (Lindsay, Gramsu, McLaughlin, Hood, & Espie, 1987), and more effective than behavior therapy alone (Butler et al., 1991). Others have found cognitive, cognitive-behavioral, and behavioral therapies equally effective (White, Keenam, & Brooks, 1992). A number of researchers have demonstrated the differential efficacy of cognitive and cognitive-behavioral interventions compared with pharmacological treatments in the treatment of generalized anxiety.

In addition, Power et al. (1990) found that the clients undergoing cognitive treatment exhibited better maintenance of gains than those involved in drug treatments.

Phobias. Two types of phobias (simple and social) have received the most intensive study. For simple phobias, the treatment of choice is usually in vivo exposure (Emmelkamp, 1994; Marshall, Bristol, & Barbaree, 1992; Rachman & Levitt, 1988). There is little evidence to suggest that anything beyond exposure helps, although some evidence from studies indicates that applied relaxation is a useful addition (Ost, Fellenius, & Sterner, 1991; Ost, Sterner, & Felleneus, 1989). Gelernter et al. (1991) found that treatment gains were better maintained following cognitive-behavioral interventions than with pharmacotherapy. Cognitive therapies of social phobias were more effective than supportive therapies (Heimberg et al., 1990). Social phobias have somewhat of a different clinical picture in their emphasis on fear and avoidance of social situations. Emmelkamp and Scholing (1990) reviewed the literature on social phobias and concluded that exposure was as effective as cognitive therapy (Mattick, Peters, & Clarke, 1989; Scholing & Emmelkamp, 1993a, 1993b); self-instruction was as effective as rational emotive therapy (RET; Emmelkamp, Mersch, Vissia, & Van-der-Helm, 1985); social skills training may be better than desensitization alone (Scholing & Emmelkamp, 1989); and individualized treatment might not be any better than treatment packages applied uniformly to all clients (Mersch, Emmelkamp, & Lips, 1991).

Panic disorder and agoraphobia. Some of the empirically supported treatments for panic disorder are similar to those found to be useful for other anxiety disorders. For example, exposure in vivo seems superior to imaginal exposure (Emmelkamp & Wessels, 1975), exposure alone seems superior to cognitive therapy (Emmelkamp, Brilman, Kuipers, & Mersch, 1986), and the effects of exposure seem to last (Burns, Thorpe, & Cavallero, 1986). Applied relaxation (having clients first notice anxious sensations and then use relaxation techniques to cope with these before onset of panic attack) has also been found to be effective (Ost, 1988), although not more so than cognitive therapy (Clark, 1991). Problem solving may be useful in addition to exposure treatment, but the effects do not seem to stand alone (Emmelkamp, 1994). Moreover, assertiveness training seems to help improve assertiveness, but it does not significantly impact anxiety and avoidance beyond effects attributable to exposure (Emmelkamp, 1980). Marital therapy with couples in which one is agoraphobic does not seem any more effective than individual treatment.

Some research indicates that cognitive approaches are effective with panic disorder (Ruiter, Rijken, Garssen, & Kraaimaat, 1989). Cognitive approaches seem at least equally as effective as other cognitive behavioral and behavioral approaches (Bouman & Emmelkamp, 1993; Clark, 1991). Sokol et al. (1989) found that focused cognitive therapy totally eliminated panic attacks, with results still evident at a 1-year follow-up. Beck et al. (1992) found that cognitive therapy was superior to nonspecific supportive therapies with panic disorders. At the end of treatment, 70% of those treated with focused cognitive therapy were panic free, but only 25% of the supportive therapy clients were panic free. Cognitive therapy for panic disorders has also been found to be superior to both applied relaxation and imipramine drug therapy (Clark, Salkovskis, Hackmann, Middleton, & Gelder, 1992). Cognitive therapy also seems helpful in treating the catastrophic cognitions that can be a part of panic attacks. In a clinical trial, over 85% of clients treated with panic control therapy (PCT; a combination of behavioral coping techniques including relaxation training) were panic-free at the end of treatment, as compared to 50% of those treated with alprazolam, and 35% treated with placebo and wait list controls (Barlow et al., 1989).

Obsessive-compulsive disorder. The efficacy of treatment for obsessive-compulsive disorders is well documented (Kasvikis & Marks, 1988; Visser, Hoekstra, & Emmelkamp, 1992). Exposure and response prevention of the accompanying rituals are the important components of successful treatment (Foa, Steketee, Grayson, Turner, & Latimer, 1984). Longer periods of exposure are more effective than shorter periods (Emmelkamp, 1994), outpatient and inpatient treatments are relatively equal in efficacy (Hout, Emmelkamp, Kraaykamp, & Griez, 1988), and client-guided treatment seems equally as effective as therapist-guided intervention (Emmelkamp, van Linden, van den Heuvell, Ruphan, & Sanderman, 1989). Emmelkamp, Visser, and Hoekstra (1988) and Emmelkamp and Beens (1991) both found that cognitive therapy was as effective as *in vivo* exposure. Behavioral treatments seem to effectively reduce compulsive behaviors, but are less effective in reducing ruminations. Marshall and Segal (1990) suggested that behavioral therapies are no more effective in the treatment of obsessive-compulsive disorder than drug treatment in the long run. Christensen, Hadzi-Pavlovic, Andrews, and Mattick (1987) found that the therapeutic results gained from drug treatment of these disorders are not maintained.

The efficacy of treatment does seem to depend on a number of diagnostic characteristics. For example, checking compulsions have a less favorable prognosis than those that involve washing (Boulougouris, Rabavillas, & Stefanis, 1977). Similarly, those clients with symptoms that are more severe and of longer duration have a less favorable prognosis (Basoglu, Lax, Kasvcikis, & Marks, 1988; Hoogduin, Duivenvoorden, Schapap, & de Haan, 1989).

In conclusion, the current outcome literature suggests that with certain client-presenting problems, some treatments are more helpful than others. These findings support the notion that it is clinically useful to match client-presenting problems with empirically established treatments. Unfortunately, the outcome literature has only focused on those client disorders that can be reliably classified. Many of the presenting concerns seen by practicing counselors do not fit into these categories. In addition, many of the diagnostic pictures presented by clients do not fit single categories. Thus, although the notion of problem-treatment matching is conceptually appealing, there is considerable progress to be made before it becomes the primary basis for clinical decision making.

Relational matching. An area of increasing research interest is represented by studies investigating the match between therapist and client interpersonal styles. This research has led to the development of the interactional models of the counseling relationship previously discussed. This research has been influenced by the construct of complementarity as originally proposed by Leary (1957) and Bateson (1972). Although the two views of complementarity differ in definition, both models suggest that when the interpersonal styles of counselor and client fit together a stable relationship is established. The fit is usually considered along the dimensions of control and dominance and affilitative and friendly relationship styles. When the styles do not fit, interpersonal instability exists (for a more detailed explanation of complementarity, see Claiborn & Lictenberg, 1989, or Sexton & Whiston, 1994).

Both Kiesler and Watkins (1989) and Tracey and Hayes (1989) found moderate levels of therapeutic complementarity to be related to positive therapeutic outcome. Andrews (1990) found that those client-counselor dyads less likely to improve were characterized by anti-complementary styles on the control and dominance dimension and reciprocity on the affiliation dimension. Henry et al. (1990) was able to distinguish good (complementary styles) from poor outcome (lacking complementarity) counseling dyads. Other studies indicate complementarity may not only be important in distinguishing good and bad sessions (Friedlander, Thibodeau, & Ward, 1985; Tracey, 1987), but may also be a factor in the establishment of the therapeutic alliance (Tracey, 1986) and the retention of clients in therapy (Tracey, 1985).

Integrating Research and Practice: Conclusions and Implications

This extensive database of counseling outcome studies has produced several consistent patterns that appear in the wide range of studies across numerous client types. When examining the findings of individual studies, there appear to be numerous contradictions. However, there are trends across studies that are quite robust. Each of these trends has implications for both practice and education. What follows is a list of general conclusions that can be reached from the current data on counseling outcome. Our conclusions are based on the best of what outcome research has to offer once methodological factors are taken into account. Like Orlinsky et al. (1994), we believe these conclusions to be relatively stable trends that have stood the test of time.

1. The notion that some client variable may directly influence outcome of counseling is certainly appealing. Unfortunately, there is little support to suggest any one characteristic may directly enhance or diminish outcome. Research investigations of the interaction between the client, counselor, and treatment have produced results that can be applied to practice. In light of the limited nature of the data, however, it seems unwise to base counseling relationships or treatment interventions on simple client counselor characteristics. Effective counseling is a complex interaction of personality, process, and intervention.

2. There is no question that the counselor's therapeutic skills are an important component in effective counseling. These skills are not necessarily related to experience, profession, or type of training. Defining therapeutic skill has, in fact, been confused by a mixture of loosely related constructs. Beutler et al. (1994) suggested that one can draw three conclusions: (a) skillfulness is associated with effectiveness in various treatment models, (b) skill is distinct from experience and compliance with a therapy model, and (c) criteria-based training in specific therapeutic procedures tends to increase levels of counselor skill and competence.

In addition, no single treatment, regardless of its skillful delivery, may fit all clients. Results of recent studies suggest that certain clients respond better to the manual-guided treatment than other clients. It may be that therapists need multiple treatment protocols to match with different clients. However, as suggested by Person (1989), no degree of technical competence can overcome the need to be interpersonally skillful. Beyond specific therapist skills, it seems as if therapeutic style (directive vs. nondirective, complementary vs. anti-complementary) may be differentially important with certain kinds of clients at certain stages of counseling. As in the study of other variables, research that considers the interaction among various therapist-client-modality elements seems most promising.

3. The growing research evidence suggests that the counseling relationship is critical to the ultimate success. The relationship should not be viewed simplistically but rather as complex, multidimensional, and best represented by a host of relatively new theoretical models. Historically, we have viewed relational characteristics as absolute, believing that there was one correct style of empathy, warmth, and respect. We now know that these characteristics only have an impact when the client perceives that they are evident. As all clients are different, the implication is that we must consider these counselor-offered characteristics as relative rather than absolute constructs (Sexton & Whiston, 1994). Therefore, what is empathetic depends not solely on the action of the counselor, but more on what clients interpret as empathetic. In addition, research indicates that empathy is multidimensional, requiring further discrimination in research and practice. Bachelor's (1988) model of four distinct styles of empathy (cognitive, affective, sharing, and nutrient) may be a useful beginning for better understanding the value of empathy.

The preponderance of the empirical evidence suggests that the counseling relationship is much more complex than a single set of counselor-offered conditions. There seem to be personal characteristics exhibited by both counselor and client that promote an emotional connection that facilitates a therapeutic relationship. It further appears that these personal reactions must be mutual and reciprocal. In addition, it seems clear that an alignment regarding therapeutic goals and tasks is important. How and if that alignment is established currently seems to relate to the degree to which the client views the counselor as being a credible helper. Certain interpersonal patterns that connect clients and counselor have been found to promote effective counseling. Complementary patterns may be important for establishing the relationship, and a mismatch of positions may actually facilitate therapeutic change in the middle sections of therapy.

4. Many outcome studies fail to consider that therapy is a dynamic process with various stages. At each stage, different types of relationships are therapeutic, different techniques may be important, and different experiences can be helpful. A few studies have considered the stage of the relationship. DeRubeis et al. (1990) found, for example, that improvement in dysfunctional cognitions from the initial to middle stages, but not from middle to the end, predicted improvement in short-term cognitive therapy. Klee, Abeles, and Muller (1990) found that those clients who improved the most increasingly contributed to the therapeutic alliance as therapy progressed. Tracey (1987) found that in successful cases of time-limited counseling, both clients and counselors initiated topics more in the first and last thirds of treatment and less in the middle third. Unsuccessful cases, on the other hand, maintained stable levels of topic initiation. In a later study, Tracey (1989) also found satisfaction with counseling to follow a similar pattern. Successful cases were marked by a curvilinear pattern of client and therapist satisfaction (high-low-high). Furthermore, DeRubeis and Feeley (1990) found that client adherence to treatment assignments was only important in the initial stages of cognitive-behavioral treatment.

A number of models have been developed that propose the stage of therapy to be of primary importance. Tracey (1993) suggested that it is important to take a process approach, using those techniques and relational positions that are appropriate for the beginning, middle, and end of therapy. He proposed a stage-based model of interactional counseling. Prochaska (1991) suggested that clients go though stages of change whether in counseling or not. Those clients in the early stages (pre-contemplation and contemplation) should receive dramatically different interventions than those in the final stages of action and maintenance. Based on studies of smokers, Prochaska, Velicer, DiClemente, and Fava (1988) found that those clients in pre-contemplation stage of change are unlikely to take any specific action toward problem solution. It is not that these clients are resisting help, but rather they are not ready for that help. Matching stages of client change with therapeutic intervention may help us more accurately intervene with clients.

A common theme throughout the outcome literature suggests that counseling is a dynamic, not a static process. The implication for the practitioner is twofold. First, a map or model of counseling that can be used to guide the counseling process seems essential. One suggestion, offered by Prochaska (1991), argued that counseling interventions should be congruent with the stages of change clients go through. In this review, as well as in other presentations, we have proposed a process-based model to guide practice (Whiston & Sexton, 1993). Second, the efficacy of many techniques seems to depend on when in counseling they are used. Therefore, it seems that practitioners need to change relational style, role, and structure as the stages of counseling unfold. Relevant research integrated into one of the models proposed above might guide the selective application of techniques.

5. Effective counseling is based on a range of established and tested interventions. There is a range of specific, well-documented treatments with established efficacy that can be used with various client problems. These treatments are not necessarily theory-based approaches, but are specific interventions designed for specific client problems. Many of these treatments are now based on manuals that specifically guide the clinician in successful implementation. Although treatment manuals have disadvantages, they do seem to significantly decrease the variance in outcome that can be attributed to the therapist. A major consideration should be, however, the skillful application of techniques that have established records with the particular client problem.

Treatment manuals could be an important educational tool to help students develop a range of effective counseling interventions. Rather than relying on the theories to guide practice, students could be taught to match client characteristics with treatments that have demonstrated effectiveness in that area. Using manuals as the basis of learning interventions could increase student-counselors' skill and prepare them for practice.

6. There is considerable evidence to suggest that various models of counseling (e.g., cognitive, experiential, behavioral, dynamic) are effective. However, when these schools of counseling are compared, they seem to be equivalent in their effect on counseling outcome. These findings have led to a breakdown in the traditional focus on school-specific therapies. It appears that two trends have emerged. The first is a movement toward identifying the common factors that are evident in all successful therapies. Largely undefined, these factors seem to capture a significant amount of the variance in treatment outcome. The second trend is that researchers are increasingly focusing on the study of client-treatment protocol matching. Clients with certain presenting problems are treated with various packaged interventions that may have a behavioral, cognitive, or dynamic focus. Thus, outcome studies can now provide a useful guide for determining a treatment of choice for certain well-defined presenting concerns.

7. There is probably no other element of counseling more consistently related to successful outcome than the quality of the relationship between the client and counselor. What is therapeutic about that relationship has been difficult to determine. We now know that the counseling relationship is more than counselor offered facilitative-based conditions. Successful counseling occurs in the context of a therapeutic relationship in which the participants have mutual feelings of empathy and affiliation and clear and agreed-on goals that are accomplished in collaborative ways. Expanding one's view of the counseling relationship allows a practitioner to better understand what needs to occur as a foundation of successful intervention. A broad view of the relationship is captured in three interactive models of the relationship. We think that each of these models (working alliance, social influence, and interactional) have enough empirical support that they can defensibly serve as a foundation of both practice and education.

8. The research evidence presented here suggests that counseling might be enhanced by going beyond the typical demographic and diagnostic characteristics gathered in assessment. It is important to explore the clients' presenting problems, levels of distress, and their

relational style. Careful matching of client and counselor attributes and values and beliefs accounts for up to 50% of the variance in counseling. Incorporating this matching information can only be done if these characteristics are formally assessed (Beutler, 1989). Beutler, Consoli, and Williams (1995) suggest that client problems might best be understood on a continuum from simple to complex. Simple problems are those that arise from situational difficulties stemming from external factors, complex problems are related to characterological problems that involve enduring personal and interpersonal patterns. Simple problems seem best addressed by teaching, learning, and problem-solving methods, whereas complex problems may require more in-depth examination and treatment of pattern change (Nelson & Allstetter-Neufeldt, 1996).

9. Counseling outcome research has been able to identify a number of protocols that are particularly effective with certain client problems. We can now say that depression, anxiety, panic disorders, and obsessive-compulsive disorders are better treated by some techniques rather than others. This knowledge can become part of the counseling practitioner's treatment planning procedure. It is unfortunate that we have been unable to determine the most effective treatments for other less specific problems. As outcome research grows more sophisticated, we will most likely become even better at identifying the most important treatments for an array of client concerns.

10. Counseling is generally a helpful process, however, it is not always benign. A significant number of clients get worse as a result of counseling. It seems that what is most important about the counselor's role is the skill with which he or she engages the client in a therapeutic relationship, implements tested therapeutic protocols, and terminates the relationship. Skillfulness seems to involve focusing the conversations in therapy, addressing the presenting concerns directly, structuring and guiding therapy, and successfully matching client and treatment.

These skillful characteristics seem significantly more important than many of the simple professional and personal characteristics often emphasized in counselor education. Demographic and personal characteristics of the counselor seem to have little impact on outcome. Counselor experience, professional affiliation, and professional training all depend on the skilled implementation of counseling. Personal development, self-awareness, and personal therapy of the counselor are not nearly as important as skill level. It is probably the case that such personal characteristics become important if they seriously impair the counselor's ability to skillfully conduct therapy. Thus, the time and resources often devoted to personal awareness and development, the emphasis on personal therapy, and the focus on the self during counselor training are really not defensible unless coupled with an even greater emphasis on enhancing therapeutic skillfulness.

This chapter illustrates the way in which many of the outcome research trends can be applied to counseling practice and education. Although the primary focus here has been on individual counseling, we believe many of these trends speak to the broad principles of behavior change. Thus, these implications apply in a wide variety of counseling approaches. In the next chapter, we focus on the specific practice of career counseling. Like individual counseling, there are important trends that can be used to guide the practice and understand the practice of career counseling.

CHAPTER 5

Career Interventions From a Research Perspective

Historically, career counseling and assisting clients with their career development has been a fundamental element of the counseling field's preventative focus. Although some may claim that the profession of counseling is drifting away from career counseling, there are numerous indications that many clients need assistance with their career planning. Several national reports suggest that the need for career guidance among secondary students remain largely unheeded (Herr & Cramer, 1996). Consistently, surveys have indicated that around half of U.S. college students report needing assistance with choosing a career. Only 36% of adults report they are in occupations where they made a conscious choice and followed a definite plan (Hoyt & Lester, 1994). Even the federal government has begun to understand that students need assistance, and it recently funneled money into school-to-work transition programs.

There are also predictions that more people will be needing assistance with their careers because of changes in the work world. Our society is constantly changing; rarely does an individual begin a job in early adulthood and retire from that same job at the age of 65. Developments in technology will create new jobs and even new fields. Many of the jobs that exist today will not exist in 20 years.

Technological advances will mean that some workers will lose their jobs. Predictions are that unskilled workers will have a difficult time obtaining any type of employment. Children need to be prepared for the job market of tomorrow and adults need to develop career planning skills for a changing world. These changes in our society will demand more of both counselors and researchers if we are to develop and provide career counseling techniques that will meet those needs.

We contend that effective career counseling builds on the factors already identified in Chapters 3 and 4 (therapeutic relationships, contracts, and matched interventions). Consistent with other scholars (Hackett, 1993; Imbimbo, 1994; Krumboltz, 1993), we do not see an artificial boundary between personal and career counseling. Using the research on effective counseling as a foundation, this chapter will focus on those interventions developed to assist individuals with career issues. Our focus will include a broad spectrum of techniques related to facilitating career development, assisting in effective decision making, and helping resolve career difficulties. We include studies related to career counseling, career guidance, and vocational assistance. Consistent with Spokane (1991), we will use the term *career interventions* to describe the extensive array of career techniques that includes, but is not limited to, career counseling, workshops, classes, and computer applications.

Given the current state of career intervention research, we believe there are three salient questions. First, Are career interventions effective? The next logical question is, What factors influence outcome? Finally we address, Does the effectiveness of career interventions vary depending on the career outcome?

Are Career Interventions Effective?

Meta-analytic reviews suggest that the broad range of career counseling interventions are indeed effective. The magnitude of these effects does vary depending on which review and when the analysis was conducted. Two seminal meta-analytic reviews, by Spokane and Oliver (1983) and Oliver and Spokane (1988), clearly identified large effects attributable to career interventions (ES = .85, .82, respectively). Their review included over 30 years of career research and involved some 7,311 participants. Whiston, Sexton, and Lasoff (1996) extended on their earlier work and analyzed recent research

(1983–1995). They also found career interventions to be effective, but to a lesser degree (ES = .37). When analyzing the results of both meta-analyses, Oliver, Whiston, Sexton, Lasoff, and Spokane (1996) concluded that career interventions have a moderate effect on outcome.

Qualitative research reviews also indicate that career interventions are effective (Holland, Magoon, & Spokane, 1981; Krumboltz, Becker-Haven, & Burnett, 1979; Myers, 1986). A review of recent career research found that 83% of the studies reported positive effects as a result of an intervention (Sexton, Whiston, Bleuer, & Walz, 1995). In addition, a review of career development interventions for college students found that a wide variety of approaches were being used to foster career development on college campuses, and that in general these interventions were effective (Pickering & Vacc, 1984). Fretz (1981) contended that "the evidence suggests that myriad, diverse interventions result in small yet consistently detectable gains" (p. 77). He further suggested that we move away from the simple question of whether career counseling is effective to questions related to what treatment factors work with which clients.

What Factors Influence Outcome?

In attempting to identify the factors that contribute to the effectiveness of career interventions, researchers have primarily investigated client characteristics, counselor factors, and types of interventions. Although a number of factors are related to career outcome, it will soon become apparent that only a limited number of these variables have a substantial impact.

Client Characteristics

Identifying significant client characteristics in the career area has been as fruitless as it was in outcome research in individual counseling. The major meta-analyses of career interventions found neither the type of client nor the age of the client to be a significant contributor to effect size (Oliver & Spokane, 1988; Whiston et al., 1996). It does seem, however, that career interventions are more effective at some age levels than at others. Oliver and Spokane (1988) found that career counseling was effective with college students, but was even more effective with junior-high students and high-school students. On the other hand, Whiston et al. (1996) found that career interventions were most effective with college students and adults. In both studies, the effect sizes for elementary students were extraordinarily low. An important point, however, is these negative findings are based on only two studies. It is disturbing that since 1950, only two experimental studies have examined how to effectively intervene with elementary school childrens' career development.

There is also research evidence to suggest that career interventions can be effective with diverse populations. Three of these studies found that career interventions had a positive influence on minority clients' career maturity or development (Dunn & Veltman, 1989; Henry, Bardo, & Henry, 1992; Rodriguez & Blocher, 1988). Furthermore, Rodriguez and Blocher found that a traditional career program was just as effective as one designed specifically for minority students. A career counseling program for students with learning disabilities was also found to increase the students' career maturity (Hutchinson, Freeman, Downey, & Kilbreath, 1992). However, career workshops for academically talented students had mixed results. For example, a three-session workshop focused on values had a consistent influence on the development of identity but not on the development of purpose (Kerr & Erb, 1991). In another study, gifted students who attended a one-day workshop were more likely to talk with others about their career development but were not more likely than a control group to use career information (Kerr & Ghrist-Priebe, 1988).

A limited number of psychological characteristics of career clients have been studied. One of the few studies in this area explored client self-efficacy (Eden & Aviram, 1993). They found that, for those individuals who entered the workshop with low general self-efficacy, a job-search workshop did significantly increase the probability of finding employment, but it was not likely to have an impact on those who entered with high general self-efficacy. They also found that the proportion of the increase in job search activities was greater for those who entered the workshop with low general self-efficacy compared with those with high general self-efficacy. The authors concluded that because all participants did not benefit equally, counselors should make sure there is a match between the client and the type of career counseling. Another study examined whether the client characteristic of precounseling motivation had an influence on outcome (Dorn, 1989). The findings, once again, were consistent with research in individual counseling, where the level of motivation before career counseling was not related to outcome.

Some clients may respond better to computer-assisted career interventions than others. Lenz, Reardon, and Sampson (1993) investigated the effect of selected client characteristics (i.e., gender, personality, level of identity, degree of differentiation) on clients' evaluation of SIGI-Plus (a computerized career guidance system). Surprisingly, only personality had a significant influence on the clients' ratings. Lenz et al. found that clients who had higher scores on the Social and Enterprising scales tended to rate the system's contribution to their self and occupational knowledge lower. It may be that people-oriented clients would find career interventions that involve interacting with people more helpful than computer interventions.

Identifying the critical client characteristics that influence successful career counseling has been difficult. It may be that, much like individual counseling, simple identification of client characteristic does not capture the complexity of the process. There are those in the career area, most notably Fretz (1981), who have argued that research must examine the interaction between client attributes and types of interventions.

Counselor Factors

One of the unique questions studied in the career intervention area is whether or not a counselor is even needed. Several studies have examined whether a counselor is needed or whether solitary activities, such as using a computer or reading occupational information, are sufficient. In a review of career interventions with college students, Pickering and Vacc (1984) found that self-help interventions that did not involve a counselor were the least effective interventions. The need for counselor involvement has also been supported by studies analyzing computer interventions. A number of studies have indicated that computer-plus-counseling is more effective than computer-only interventions (Garis & Niles, 1990; Marin & Splete, 1991; Niles & Garis, 1990).

Building on the research indicating that the combined effect of computer use and counseling is more effective than computer use alone, Niles (1993) investigated when it was most efficacious for a counselor to intervene when using a computer-assisted career guidance system. He examined the differences among strategies that prepare the client to use the system (preintervetion), interventions that occur during the use of the computer system (enroute), and strategies that focus on planning after completing the system (postintervention). Regarding decreasing career indecision, the findings indicated that the postintervention strategy clients had less indecision than the control group. In the area of enjoying working with computers, the enroute strategy group reported more enjoyment than did the postintervention group.

Attempts have been made to see if the level of counselor experience was important. Two meta-analyses indicated that counselor training level had some influence on outcome (Oliver & Spokane, 1988; Whiston et al., 1996). Both studies, however, found that counselors in training were more effective than experienced counselors. There are several plausible explanations for this result. One is that experience is not a useful construct, because having more experience does not guarantee that the counselor is more skilled. Another explanation might have to do with treatment integrity (see Chapter 2). It may be more likely that counselors in training are part of a well-formulated research study because of their proximity to university settings. A common method of ensuring treatment integrity is providing training to the counselors. Thus, the counselors in training may have received more specific training in these career interventions than the experienced counselors out in the field. In conclusion, it seems that we need to know more about the effects of training level, experience, and level of counselor skill.

A few other counselor activities have been explored in terms of their relationship with career outcome. Note-taking during a career counseling session did not effect perceptions of social influence characteristics, but clients had a greater willingness to continue with counselors who did not take notes (Miller, 1992). Counselor self-disclosure in training for job interviewing did not lead to better outcome (Donley, Horan, & DeShong, 1989).

In conclusion, research on counselor variables has not produced any conclusive results. Fortunately for counselors, results suggest that having a counselor involved in the process is better than not having a counselor involved. However, understanding how counselors can positively impact career outcome is far from clear. As we have said repeatedly in this book, the most useful findings are related to the interaction among client, counselor, and treatment.

Types of Interventions

Although very few factors have been found to be related to career outcome, the type of intervention does have a significant influence. In fact, in (Whiston et al., 1996) meta-analysis, type of treatment was the only significant factor related to outcome. Furthermore, they found that individual counseling is the most effective treatment modality. They found that the other treatments (e.g., workshops, classes, computer interventions, counselor-free interventions) were not significantly different from each other. The conclusion that individual career counseling is efficacious was also supported by the effect size of .74 found in the Oliver and Spokane (1988) study.

Another way of determining the value of a type of treatment is to examine the number of sessions needed for career counseling to be effective. Along this line, some researchers have been interested in the ratio of effect size to number of sessions. Individual counseling has consistently emerged as the most effective intervention per unit of time involved (Oliver & Spokane, 1988; Whiston et al., 1996). Nevertheless, group and class interventions reach larger groups of individuals at one time. Oliver and Spokane (1988) found that when the cost of the counselor's professional time was incorporated into the calculation, then workshops, which involved the largest number of participants per counselor, proved to be most cost-effective. Whiston et al. (1996) found that group test interpretation and computer treatments were the most cost effective. Debate over whether it is most effective to deliver career counseling individually, in groups, or in classes will probably continue. Swanson (1995) concluded that group and individual career counseling may be differentially effective for different types of clients.

A fascinating article by Kirschner, Hoffman, and Hill (1994) provides unique insight into specific interventions a counselor performs in individual career counseling. Using a single-case design, this study incorporated methodologies currently used in process and outcome research in individual psychotherapy. At the end of seven sessions the client had attained her career goals and had increased both her career exploration and her exploration stress. Furthermore, at the 18-month follow up, the client's exploration stress had decreased and for the most part she maintained her other positive changes. They also examined counselor intuitions, which are the aspects of counselings on which the counselor intends to focus. The most helpful counselor intentions were to give information and support, clarify meaning, attend to feelings, promote insight, reinforce change, challenge, and build and foster the relationship. Kirschner et al. studied the client's reaction to various counselor intentions at different stages in the counseling process. The first session was characterized by intentions to structure the counseling, assessment of the client's problem, and provision of support, and the remaining sessions were characterized by intentions of feeling, insight, and challenge. The researchers followed up with this client 5 years after the career counseling, and the client reported that the career counseling had had a profound influence on her life.

Another study found that precounseling perceptions of what clients preferred in career counseling and what they anticipated would occur were not always the same (Galassi, Crace, Martin, James, & Wallace, 1992). They found that client preferences were that career counseling should consist of about three sessions and focus on specific career plans and decision making; and the results of the counseling should be a clearer sense of direction. Clients preferred a task-focused process but anticipated a person-focused process. In addition, clients anticipated that testing would be part of the career counseling, but were often unsure of the benefits of the testing. These results would indicate that it would be beneficial to use a more task-oriented approach and explain the purpose of any testing that is performed.

Nevo's (1990) results were consistent with such a task-focused approach. He found that a client's perceptions of the counselor as having been helpful in choosing a career alternative, making a decision, defining one's abilities and interests, and organizing one's thinking to be important. Interestingly, client satisfaction with the career counseling was not related to the counselor being a good communicator and listener.

Although computer activities were not found to be as effective as individual counseling, there is a growing interest in evaluating computerized career interventions. From 1950 to 1982, only three studies analyzed computer usages in career counseling, whereas from 1983 to

1995, nine computer studies were published. The increase in research probably reflects the expanded use of computers in career counseling. In Sexton et al.'s (1995) review, five out of six studies indicated that either SIGI or DISCOVER had a positive influence on career decidedness. They did not find computer interventions to have a consistently positive influence on career maturity. One can conclude from the Sexton et al. review that SIGI and DISCOVER are most appropriately used to facilitate making an effective career decision and should be used when it is developmentally appropriate for clients. It is clear that we need more research that examines the client's developmental stage and the appropriateness of the interventions.

One study that did examine the student's developmental stage (exploration, crystallization, choice, or clarification) was Mau and Jepsen (1992). Not only did they examine the client's stage, but also how the stage, and the client's decision-making style interacted with instruction in two different methods of decision-making strategies. This study compared two decision-making strategies: the Elimination by Aspects Strategy (EBA; the decision maker looks for a choice of action that is "good enough" rather than best and eliminates options) and the Subjective Expected Utility (SEU; the decision maker specifies desired outcomes and evaluates each alternative until the right choice is made). The results suggested that the client's stage in the career decision-making process and his or her style of decision making should be taken into account when selecting decision-making strategies. Students with a rational decision-making style showed less anxiety and indecision and showed greater certainty in their choice. However, students overall had a higher measure of cognitive complexity if they were taught the SEU strategy. In addition, students in the exploration stage who were taught the EBA strategy engaged in more searches for information than the control group.

It may be that working with parents can have a positive effect on children's career development. In a unique approach, rather than counseling the students, Kush and Cochran (1993) and Palmer and Cochran (1988) worked with parents and provided them with instruction on helping their adolescent children. The results of these studies indicated that this approach had a positive effect on the adolescents' career development and sense of agency.

We have learned that a career intervention may not produce the expected outcome. Bodden and James (1976) found that providing occupational information decreased vocational differentiation. Vocational differentiation is the number of independent constructs available to a person in perceiving careers. Leso and Neimeyer (1991) extended on the work of Bodden and his colleagues and found that occupational information resulted in a decrease in vocational differentiation for certain clients. Participants who were instructed to use provided constructs to evaluate careers had a decrease in vocational differentiation after using occupational information. Participants who used their own personally elicited constructs to evaluate careers did not have decreases in vocational differentiation after reading occupational information. These results suggest that counselors may need to be selective rather than advising all clients to use occupational information.

Although there is consensus that personal and career counseling overlap, there is controversy concerning the degree to which they overlap and whether the focus should be more on the career end or the personal end of the continuum. Phillips, Friedlander, Kost, Specterman, and Robbins (1988) explored the specific question of whether it is more effective to focus in the personal or vocational realm in career counseling. From the perspective of the counselors, better outcomes were associated with more counseling sessions and more of a vocational rather than personal focus. Clients' satisfaction with their current occupational status was not related to whether the counseling was focused in the personal or the vocational domain. Client satisfaction was only associated with the level of experience of the counselor. Kirschner et al. (1994) examined whether there was a significant difference between the counseling intentions a counselor used in personal and in career counseling, and they found there were many similarities. The counselor in their study used intentions of support, insight, and feeling in both personal and career counseling, but in career counseling she gave more information and set limits.

Meta-analytic studies have suggested that only two variables substantially influence outcome. One of these, type of treatment, was discussed earlier. The second factor is treatment intensity. Oliver and Spokane (1988) found that intensity of treatment was the only significant contributor to outcome magnitude. Treatment intensity involves both the length and the amount of time devoted. It seems that longer career counseling activities are associated with better outcomes. A probable explanation of this finding is longer treatments are probably more comprehensive and, therefore, more likely to address the multitude of issues that surround effective career development and decision making. Consistent with the findings of the meta-analysis, McAuliffe and Fredrickson (1990) found that a long-term career group (20 sessions) was, in general, more effective than a short-term (10 sessions) and a control group. The results of this study should be interpreted cautiously, as it has some methodological problems.

In a review of career development interventions for college students, Pickering and Vacc (1984) found that long-term interventions were more successful than short-term interventions. However, short-term interventions were more popular, seemed more methodologically rigorous, and also were shown to be empirically effective.

Research findings suggest that longer is generally better. In Spokane's (1991) view, career interventions that were more comprehensive and longer (at least 10 sessions) resulted in roughly twice the beneficial effects of briefer interventions.

Does the Degree of the Change Depend on the Career Outcome?

Many scholars (Super, 1957; Vandracek, Lerner, & Schulenberg, 1986) suggest that we should select career interventions depending on the client's stage of career development. The intended outcome of a career intervention should vary depending on the developmental stage of the client. For example, increasing career information-seeking behavior may be an appropriate outcome measure when working with middle-school students; on the other hand, there may be other measures that are better if the interventions being evaluated are with dual career couples. Yet, as Myers (1986) indicated, information-seeking behavior is an outcome measure that is often used because simple counts of frequency and variety of information sources are easy to accomplish. The extent to which an outcome measure is meaningful is associated with the usefulness of the findings. There are numerous methods for classifying career outcomes (Crites, 1981; Fretz, 1981; Oliver & Spokane, 1988). In these systems two major areas emerge, career decision making and effective role functioning.

In the area of career counseling and interventions, we sometimes want to help an individual select an appropriate career and make a career decision. Therefore, it is logical that there would be outcome measures related to career decision making. Within this broad area of career decision making, the outcome measure most commonly used is not whether the client has chosen a career, but rather measuring if he or she becomes more certain or decided about their career choice. The popularity of this certainty or decided outcome category is related to a well developed and sound instrument, the Career Decision Scale (Osipow, Carney, Winer, Yanico, & Koschier, 1976), which is the most commonly used outcome measure in the career area (Sexton, 1996). We need other outcome categories, as making a career decision is not always the intended goal. For example, we would not want a career guidance intervention for third graders to result in them making a premature career decision.

The other major category of career outcome is effective role function. This includes measures of how effectively the person is functioning, such as grade point average, self-concept measures, anxiety measures, and skill performance measures. In the area of effective role functioning, the specific outcome area that has received the most interest is career maturity and development. In general, meta-analyses indicate that career interventions tend to be more effective in increasing career maturity than in influencing career decidedness (Oliver & Spokane, 1988; Whiston et al., 1996). However, this is not true for all career counseling interventions. Sexton et al. (1995) found that computer-assisted career interventions were more effective in facilitating career decidedness than they were in effecting career maturity or career development. It is important for practitioners to ask what is the intended goal of the career intervention. Sometimes, with adults, the goals are easily identified (e.g., gaining employment); however, with children and adolescents, the goal is often to increase their career maturity. In increasing career maturity, counselors must be knowledgeable about appropriate developmental levels and how to appropriately facilitate that development.

Integrating Research Into Practice: Conclusions and Implications

The history of career counseling is long and rich, reaching back to Parsons (1909). However, the history of career interventions outcome research is not as long and rich. Compared to areas such as individual counseling, there is a paucity of research to guide the practitioner in career counseling practice. The following five conclusions represent what we can confidently conclude about the current status of career interventions research.

1. In general we know that career counseling is effective. The degree to which it is effective is unclear, and recent research indicates it may not be as overwhelmingly effective as previously thought. Yet, a preponderance of evidence indicates that career counseling is truly helpful to many clients. As in individual counseling research, efforts should now be focused on understanding the elements that may contribute to that effectiveness.

2. Results of the meta-analyses in this area suggest that both the type of treatment modality and the duration of time spent counseling are the primary factors that effect outcome in career counseling. In terms of an effective type of treatment, individual counseling is the most effective. It also seems that career counseling will be more effective if it is longer and involves more sessions. Therefore, in the best of all worlds, we should see clients individually for probably at least 10 sessions. These findings make intuitive sense, as longer career counseling can be more comprehensive and allows counselors to respond to the unique needs of the individual client. Nevertheless, some counselors are in settings where providing lengthy individual counseling is not an option. In terms of cost effectiveness, workshops, group test interpretation, and computer treatments are the best types of treatment. Practitioners and researchers may want to explore the efficacy of combined approaches, where clients receive individual counseling, group test interpretation, access to appropriate computer software, and a dynamic career workshop. This approach may be both cost-effective and highly productive.

3. There is empirical evidence that in career counseling, clients prefer a task-focused rather than person-focused approach (Galassi et al., 1992). These researchers found that clients preferred career counseling to last for about three sessions, focus on specific career plans and decision making, and provide the client with a clearer sense of direction. This is consistent with Nevo's (1990) study, in which clients reported they wanted the counselor to help them

choose a career alternative, define their abilities and interests, and organize their thinking. From the client's perspective, there was no difference in outcome if the focus was in the personal realm or the vocational realm (Phillips et al., 1988).

4. Career intervention research indicates that counselors need to be sensitive to the interaction between treatment approaches and client characteristics. Fretz (1981) recommended that research look more at the interaction between client attributes and different types of treatment. Researchers are beginning to tease out some of the client–treatment interactions. There are some indications that minority clients benefit from career interventions, although we don't know which types of treatments are most effective. Job search workshops do not appear to be particularly helpful to clients with high self-efficacy, but are very helpful to clients with low self-efficacy. Clients' decision-making styles interact with different treatment strategies. In addition, there are findings that suggest reading occupational information or using one of the computer-assisted career guidance system does not have the same positive effect for all clients. Although we know that career interventions are generally effective, it is clear we need to know more about which interventions are appropriate for which clients.

The implications for counselor educators is that counselors need to be trained so that they are knowledgeable about career counseling techniques, and can choose the right technique for different clients. Students' perspectives on career counseling continue to be influenced by the historical model of test and tell. Career counseling is more complex than giving an interest inventory and telling clients what jobs they should pursue. Student counselors need to be acclimated to the current culture of career counseling, which includes a thorough induction to career interventions research.

5. We suggest that career counseling scholars follow the lead of individual counseling educators and develop treatment manuals. Developing these manuals could be helpful to researchers, practitioners, and counselor educators. Although we know individual career counseling is the most effective, we do not have specific information concerning what should take place in that counseling. The process of career counseling continues to be ill-defined. Developing treatment manuals would help counselors specify the steps and pro-

cedure of effective career counseling. Consequently, outcome research in this area would improve because manuals are invaluable in terms of monitoring treatment integrity. Without treatment manuals, the shotgun approach to career treatment continues, where there is little uniformity of treatments across different studies. Career counseling in one study may be entirely different from career counseling in another study. Career treatment manuals would foster more useful treatment comparison studies, for we would then know that we are really comparing apples and oranges.

Treatment manuals would assist practitioners and counselor educators in providing prescriptive procedures for intervening with clients. In this area there are few resources that provide procedures for career counseling. In addition, counselor educators need to teach students how to do career counseling. The career theories typically presented in classes (e.g., John Holland's and Donald Super's) address the general phenomenon of career development. Treatment manuals could bridge the gap between theory and practice. For example, students could learn Holland's theory and then learn from the manual how to counsel using the tenants of that theory. In this capacity, students would have a richer educational experience.

This chapter has summarized the findings related to the effectiveness of career interventions. We intended this summary of research on career interventions to be useful to the practitioners whose job duties are primarily related to career counseling, and also for counselors who occasionally have clients with career issues. School counselors also provide career services to students, and we hope they find this chapter and the proceeding chapter useful. In the next chapter, we will take a similar approach and examine the research base that supports school counseling.

CHAPTER 6

Working With Children: Counseling and School-Based Interventions

Currently there are more than 70,000 professional school counselors working in all levels of schools (Perry, 1993). In today's world, these counselors are faced with a myriad of student problems. Some of these problems have to do with academic and career-related issues, and others have to do with emotional or behavioral problems. The severity of student problems vary, but the problems are becoming increasingly troublesome (e.g., violence in the schools, child abuse, substance abuse). To meet those needs, school counselors are being asked to intervene both preventatively and remedially.

There is no question that many school-aged children and adolescents need some type of counseling services, which can be provided in either a school setting or a community agency. Epidemiological studies indicate that from 17% to 22% of youth under 18 years of age suffer developmental, behavioral, or emotional problems (Costell, 1989; Zill & Schoenborn, 1990). The monetary costs for these troubled children and adolescents is staggering. For example, the Institute of Medicine (1989) estimated that for just the year of 1985 $1.5 billion was spent on youths under the age of 14 with mental disorders. Thus, the preventative interventions used by school counselors could be cost effective and save considerable amounts of tax dollars.

Given school counselors' numerous responsibilities, it is important that they choose interventions that are effective. Two bodies of literature can help in this regard. First, there is a significant body of research on counseling with children. Sometimes counselors will work directly with the child and other times they will need to refer a child to an outside agency. In either case, the psychotherapy literature can be a useful resource. On this foundation, we will then review research support for the specific activities of school counselors (i.e., guidance curriculum, individual planning, response services, system support activities).

Counseling With Children and Adolescents

Counseling children and adolescents requires skills and competencies different than those needed to work with adults. This section is not geared exclusively for school counselors; it can be useful to any counselor who assists children and adolescents. The number of outcome studies on children and adolescents is somewhat smaller than the massive amount of research concerning counseling and psychotherapy outcome with adults (Kazdin, 1991). Nevertheless, there are pertinent research findings that have some important implications for professionals working with the adolescent and children population. As in preceding chapters, this review will be organized around a series of questions. The first question: Is psychotherapy with children and adolescents effective?, will be followed by Which treatment models are most effective?"

Is Psychotherapy With Children and Adolescents Effective?

There is general agreement that psychotherapy with children and adolescents is effective (Kazdin, 1991, 1993, 1994). Indications are that psychotherapy tends to be about as effective with children as it is with adults. A meta-analytic review by Casey and Berman (1985) indicated that treated children achieved outcomes about two-thirds of a standard deviation better than untreated children (ES = .71). Weisz et al.'s (1987) mean effect size was a little larger (ES = .79), with the average treated youngster doing significantly better than the nontreated child.

There is general consensus that psychotherapy for children and adolescents is effective, but we do not know what variables moderate or influence the effect (Kazdin, 1994). Indications are that research with children and adolescents is increasing, and we will know more about these factors in the coming years. One of the reasons we have such limited knowledge is that it is more difficult to conduct research with children than with adults. It is more difficult to get approval to try an experimental treatment with children. It is also more difficult to gather a sample, as consent forms must be signed by a parent or guardian. What we do know is that developmental factors need to be included in research with children (Kazdin, 1991). A treatment could be appropriate for a depressed adolescent but harmful to a depressed first grader. Hence, the interaction between client factor and types of treatment are particularly germane here.

Which Treatment Models are Most Effective?

Like the research with adults, evidence indicates that no approach or school of therapy is any more effective than another theoretical model. Nevertheless, a close examination of this body of research identifies some emerging trends. Casey and Berman (1985) found behavioral treatments to be more effective than nonbehavioral treatments, but the types of outcome measures used probably contributed to these differences. Weisz et al. (1987) also found that behavioral treatments were more effective than nonbehavioral interventions regardless of client age, therapist experience, or client problem.

Another approach that has been studied with children and adolescents is cognitive–behavioral treatment. In an impressive meta–analysis, Durlack, Fuhrman, and Lampman (1991) examined cognitive–behavioral therapy for children (ages 5 to 13). The results of this study support the contention that developmental level needs to be taken into consideration. Type or severity of problem did not have a significant influence on treatment outcome, but the cognitive–developmental level did. For example, cognitive–behavioral therapy was best suited for preadolescents (ages 11 to 13). In contrast, younger children (ages 5 to 11) did benefit from this type of counseling, but their change was only about one half as much as preadolescents. Weisz, Rudolph, Granger, and Sweeney (1992) also found that adolescents with nonclinical depressive symptoms responded significantly better to cognitive–behavioral interventions than did children younger than 12 years. At follow-up, the children younger than 12 years had retained hardly any of the positive changes made in therapy. Cognitively oriented interventions also have been found to reduce antisocial and aggressive behavior among children (Arbuthnot & Gordon, 1986; Kazdin, Bass, Siegel, & Thomas, 1989; Kazdin, Siegel, & Bass, 1992; Kendall, Ronan, & Epps, 1991).

Target and Fonagy (1994) found that psychodynamic treatments were more likely to produce better outcomes than with older children. Their research also indicated that psychodynamic treatment with children was more effective if it was also longer and more intensive (Fonagy & Target, 1994; Target & Fonagy, 1994). These researchers concluded that intervening at an early age, children with phobic symptoms, and longer and more intensive analytic treatment are the factors that are most associated with improvement.

Relationship-based therapy (approaches associated with client-centered therapy) with children and adolescents was actively researched in the 1960s and 1970s. Several of these earlier studies indicated that these nondirective approaches were effective (e.g., Persons & Pepinsky, 1966; Truax, Wargo, & Silber, 1966). Recent research indicated that relationship-based therapy has modest effects with children, but these changes were not as large as those achieved with behavioral or cognitive–behavioral approaches (Durlak, 1980; Kazdin, Esveldt-Dawson, French, & Unis, 1987). Unlike adult psychotherapy research, we know little about the nature of the therapeutic relationship with children, and we are not aware of how the relationship effects outcome.

Nontheoretical treatments of children have also been investigated. Play therapy is often the preferred method of practice for those working with young children where more verbal and cognitive approaches are more difficult. There is an abundance of literature conceptualizing play therapy, describing treatments, and illustrating cases; however, there are few controlled outcome studies. A tentative conclusion that play therapy can produce positive change can be drawn from the small number of studies in this area (Kazdin, 1994). However, a recent study did not find that the gains of play therapy persisted at the 10-week follow-up assessment (Reams & Friedrich, 1994).

Parent training is probably the most well-investigated mode of treatment in the child psychotherapy research (Kazdin, 1994). Several studies on parent training indicate that children's behavior tends to improve as a result of working with the parents (Kazdin, 1987; McMahon & Wells, 1989). The positive effects of parent training have often been found to still be evident 1 year after treatment, and one study found the benefits lasted up to 10 years after parent training (Forehand & Long, 1988). Although there are many variations in parent training, Webster-Stratton, Hollinsworth, and Kolpacoff (1989) found that programs that incorporated both group discussion and videotaped presentations tended to be more effective.

In conclusion, research indicates that psychotherapy with children is effective. This is an area where the knowledge base is expanding. For example, in the coming years, we will know more about the process of establishing a good counseling relationship with children, whether play therapy is effective, and how to effectively intervene with children and adolescents.

School Counseling Research

Many children with emotional difficulties and behavioral problems are helped by counselors working in the schools. Even though much of the work of a school counselor takes place outside of traditional individual counseling, we can ask the same series of questions: Is school counseling effective?, How effective?, What students benefit from school counseling activities?, What are the effective methods for delivering services?, and What are the characteristics of effective school counseling programs?

Is School Counseling Effective?

In general, school counseling interventions have been found to be effective in both meta-analytic and qualitative reviews. These conclusions are not, however, based on as much research as other outcome areas. There are four meta-analytic studies that have either directly or indirectly related to school counseling.

In a small and limited meta-analytic study, Sprinthall (1981) found that primary prevention programs could work. A better review of primary prevention strategies is Baker, Swisher, Nadenichek, and Popowicz's (1984) meta-analytic review. The effect sizes varied but conservative estimates of effect size were .55. In a review of personal-social counseling or psychotherapy in schools, Prout and DeMartino (1986) also found a moderate effect size (ES = .58). This review included interventions performed both by school counselors and psychologists. The final meta-analysis (Nearpass, 1990) examined counseling and guidance in high schools and found that effect sizes varied greatly depending on the activity. In conclusion, the meta-analytic reviews of school counseling research seem to indicate that school counseling interventions are in the moderate range using Cohen's (1988) method of determining the magnitude of effect size.

Qualitative reviews also indicate that school counseling activities are effective. Borders and Drury (1992) summarized 30 years of empirical work and statements from professional organizations, and concluded that school counseling interventions have a substantial impact on students' educational and personal development. Their review cited a number of studies that indicated that students who received counseling improved their academic performance, attitudes, and behaviors. In systematic qualitative reviews of outcome research in school counseling, Whiston and Sexton (1996) concluded that a broad range of activities performed by school counselors resulted in positive changes in students. They also found, however, that not all school counseling activities have been systematically investigated.

Some of the qualitative reviews of school counseling research have focused on specific student populations. In a review of studies on elementary counseling published in 1974 through 1984, Gerler (1984) concluded that counseling programs can positively influence the affective, behavioral, and interpersonal domains of children's lives. At the middle-school level, St. Clair (1989) found support for some programs and strategies used by middle-school counselors such as a behavioral management program, successful daily progress report, and self-relaxation techniques. Wilson (1986) focused specifically on research related to the effects of counselor interventions with underachieving and low-achieving students. This article only included studies where the outcome measure was grade point average (GPA), yet the results indicated that many school counseling interventions are effective with this population.

In conclusion, it appears that school counseling interventions are generally effective. It is difficult to decipher, however, the degree to which the activities are important. The reviews of school counseling research are generally positive, whereas the meta-analytic studies tend to indicate that the activities have a moderate impact on student outcome.

Which Students Benefit From School Counseling Interventions?

It is important to consider who typically uses school counseling services. Lavoritano and Segal (1992) provided information on which students are referred by teachers for counseling. For example, they found that more males than females, more children from single-parent homes, more students who had been retained, more under-achievers, and more students who had been suspended were referred for counseling. This study is somewhat of a unique case because the information comes from an agency that provides counseling services to a number of nonpublic schools. The researchers argue that their results can be generalized to students receiving counseling in a school setting. In addition, the situation studied may not be unique as some school districts are moving to privatization of school counseling services, where instead of hiring school counselors they contract with community agencies to provide counseling services.

Mahoney and Merritt (1993) examined ethnic differences in the use of school counseling. They found a much higher percentage of African American students than White students considered counselors to be important in helping them make their educational plans. Furthermore, African Americans, particularly males, were more likely to use school counseling services to overcome academic weaknesses than were Whites. They also found the same trend concerning using counseling resources for educational or job placement.

Of those students who do use school counseling services, there is some evidence that school counseling interventions may have differential effects on students at different ages. A general trend is that older students benefit more than younger students. Prout and DeMartino (1986) found that counseling interventions performed by school counselors and psychologists were more effective with secondary students than with elementary students. In addition, interventions with upper-level high school students (11th and 12th graders) were found to be more effective than interventions with younger (9th and 10th graders) high school students (Nearpass, 1990). Gerler (1984) claimed, however, there is evidence that elementary school counselors' interventions have a positive effect on elementary school students. The student level where there is the least amount of research on the effectiveness of school counseling is with middle school students (St. Clair, 1989; Whiston & Sexton, 1996). Even though there are tentative findings that older students benefit more from school counseling activities, this should not be interpreted as an endorsement for hiring only secondary school counselors. The research in this area is very limited and longitudinal studies need to be performed before we draw conclusive findings about the effects of elementary, middle, and high school counseling.

Besides age, other student characteristics have been found to have an impact on the effectiveness of school counseling interventions. For example, with low-achieving students, programs in which students volunteer to participate were more successful than programs where the students were forced to attend (Wilson, 1986). Lapan, Gysbers, Hughey, and Arni (1993) examined a conjoint language arts career-guidance unit with high school students. The language arts unit seemed to enhance learning for girls regardless of whether they were doing well in school or not. However, for boys, it only promoted learning for those already doing well in school. These results indicate that gender should be considered in classroom guidance activities.

Other student characteristics have not been found to be related to outcome. Student background characteristics or student academic variables were not found to predict middle school students' satisfaction with group counseling (Hagborg, 1993). Background characteristics that did not relate to satisfaction were student's sex, parental marital status, presence of an educational handicap, age, grade level, and socioeconomic status. A number of academic variables were also unrelated to satisfaction with the group experience, including grades, school attendance, and standardized achievement scores. These findings suggest that some of the stereotypes regarding who will view group counseling positively may not be accurate.

In summary, the outcome research in school counseling does not provide any clear indication of which students benefit from these activities. Moreover, stereotypes concerning which students will use counseling services and be satisfied may not be completely accurate. Increasingly, school counselors are being required to serve all students in a school. Questions about which students benefit from school counseling activities are probably not as important as questions about which activities assist in the development of every student.

What Are the Effective Methods
for Delivering Services?

The school counseling research is mixed on whether it is more effective to provide service primarily through group intervention or individual counseling. There are some indications that group counseling is more effective than individual counseling (Prout & DeMartino, 1986). Consistent with Prout and Demartino's (1986) meta-analysis, Wilson (1986) found some evidence that group counseling was more effective than individual counseling in increasing academic performance of underachievers and low achievers.

Other studies have found that individual counseling is more effective than group (Nearpass, 1990). Wiggins and Wiggins (1992) found that counselors who predominately used individual counseling were more effective than those counselors who predominately used classroom guidance activities. Unfortunately, none of these results were statistically analyzed. Individual counseling does not have to be lengthy to be effective. Littrell, Malia, and Vanderwood (1995) found that three approaches to brief individual counseling were effective with secondary students. In fact, they found that the least time-consuming approach, the solution-focused model, was as effective as the other approaches. Individual counseling that was contracted by a private school resulted in increases in children's perception of their scholastic competence (Lavoritano & Segal, 1992). However, individual counseling had a mixed affect on children's self-esteem, and there was no relationship between the number of counseling sessions and the degree of improvement in self-esteem. A curious outcome here was that as the individual counseling progressed, behavioral conduct (misbehaving) actually decreased (Lavoritano & Segal, 1992).

Researchers have also examined the effectiveness of classroom guidance as a modality for providing school counseling services. In a particularly well-designed study, Rathvon (1991) examined whether a test preparation unit was more effective using a classroom guidance format or a small group format. Interestingly, there was no significant difference between either of the formats. In addition, neither of the groups were significantly different from the control group. Other research has indicated that guidance curriculum activities can be successfully integrated into an academic curriculum with secondary students. A conjoint language arts and career guidance unit was positively evaluated both quantitatively (Lapan et al., 1993) and qualitatively (Hughey, Lapan, & Gysbers, 1993). School counselors and English teachers worked cooperatively to provide to high school juniors a guidance unit that gave students an opportunity to develop academic skills and explore career issues.

In conclusion, it does not appear that any of the typical formats (i.e., individual counseling, group counseling, or classroom guidance) is more effective than the others. It is most likely that school counselors need to intervene using a variety of methods. Whether it is most effective to intervene with individual counseling, group counseling, or with an entire classroom depends on a multitude of yet-to-be determined factors. It does seem that certain school counselor activities lend themselves to certain intervention modes.

What Specific Activities are Effective?

School counselors are asked to perform many activities. Previous reviews of school counseling (Borders & Drury, 1992; St. Clair, 1989; Whiston & Sexton, 1996) found that certain school activities were supported empirically, whereas other activities were not found to be effective. This discussion of activities will use Gysbers and Henderson's (1994) model as a framework to organize results, as their model appears to be the most commonly used school counseling paradigm. The model delineates four types of activities: guidance curriculum, individual planning, response services, and system support.

Guidance curriculum activities are "the center of the developmental part of the comprehensive guidance program. It contains statements as to the goals for guidance instruction and the competencies to be developed by students. The curriculum is organized by grade level; that is, a scope and sequence of learning activities for Grades K–12 is established. It is designed to serve all students and is often called classroom or group guidance" (Gysbers & Henderson, 1994, p. 140). Borders and Drury (1992) claimed that there is empirical support for the effectiveness of classroom guidance activities. However, in a comprehensive review of current school counseling research, Whiston and Sexton (1996) did not find clear empirical support of classroom/guidance activities.

Although Whitson and Sexton (1996) did not identify any clear research trends in classroom guidance activities at the middle and high school levels, they did identify some trends at the elementary level. None of the studies included in their review clearly indicated that elementary classroom guidance programs increased self-esteem. Interestingly, the studies suggested that classroom guidance activities at the elementary level did have an impact on achievement. It is important to note, however, that the findings related to the effect on academic achievement are based on only two studies (Hadley, 1988; Lee, 1993).

Research published primarily in the 1970s provides some insight into other effective activities. Baker et al's. (1984) meta-analysis found that programs that emphasized career maturity enhancement, communication skills training, and deliberate psychological education tended to be effective. Programs that emphasized cognitive coping skills training, moral education, substance abuse prevention, and blended values clarification with other strategies had smaller effect sizes.

Individual planning activities are designed to assist students in developing and implementing their personal, educational, and career plans (Gysbers & Henderson, 1994). Whiston and Sexton (1996) found that the majority of investigations into individual planning activities focused on career development. The results of these reports indicated that individual planning interventions can have a positive impact on the development of students' career plans. These successes in career counseling activities seem to apply equally to students with a range of exceptionalities (i.e., minority, learning disabled, and gifted students). In addition, two studies found that adolescents' career development can be facilitated by instructing parents on methods for assisting their children in the career area (Kush & Cochran, 1993; Palmer & Cochran, 1988).

Responsive services, another component of Gysbers and Henderson's (1994) model, is composed of activities designed to provide special assistance to students facing problems that interfere with their healthy personal, social, or educational development. Whiston and Sexton (1996) found the majority of current school counseling studies were classified as responsive services and involved interventions with students who were currently facing academic and personal problems.

Of the wide variety of interventions studied in this responsive services area, some notable trends emerged (Whiston & Sexton, 1996). First, studies indicated that social skills training can be helpful to special needs students (Ciechalski & Schmidt, 1995; Utay & Lampe, 1995; Verduyn, Lord, & Forrest, 1990). Social skills training was found to be effective with children with general disabilities, learning disabilities, and behavioral problems, and with gifted students. This trend is also supported by research published primarily in the 1970s, which found interpersonal skills training was generally effective with elementary students (Gerler, 1984). The efficacy of classroom-based social-competence programs is also supported in the work of Weissberg, Caplan, and Harwood (1991). They concluded that the short-term benefits of social skills training has been established for preschool, elementary, middle, and high school aged children. They further asserted that we need to develop comprehensive and multiyear interventions that may produce long-term preventive effects.

The benefits of parent training and family support programs are well established in the counseling and psychotherapy outcome research (Kazdin, 1994; Weissberg et al., 1991). School counseling research supports group counseling as an effective method of helping students adjust to family difficulties (Omizo & Omizo, 1988; Rose & Rose, 1992) and working with the families as a way to assist students (Morrison, Olivos, Domingues, Gomez, & Lena, 1993; Smith, 1994). In addition, there are indications that parental involvement is significantly related to the effectiveness of the counseling with low and underachieving students (Wilson, 1986).

There also is empirical support for peer counseling and peer mediation programs both at the elementary and secondary level (Borders & Drury, 1992; Whiston & Sexton, 1996). Morey, Miller, Rosen, and Fulton (1993) found that students who were self-referred reported greater overall satisfaction than students who were referred by teachers or a counselor. The findings also indicated that peer counselor training needs to include empathetic listening and understanding skills, as well as training in problem identification and problem-solving strategies. Furthermore, higher peer counseling ratings were associated with an emphasis on improving relationship difficulties that included relationship problems both at home and at school.

The system support component of a school counseling program consists of management activities that establish, maintain, and enhance the total guidance program. Along this line, consultation activities have also been found to be an effective school counseling activity. Gerler (1984) concluded that consultation with teachers was an effective method of influencing elementary school children's behavior. Furthermore, Borders and Drury (1992) found consultation activities (e.g., consultation with teachers, school administrators, and parents) to be effective at both elementary and secondary levels.

In conclusion, school counselors provide a variety of services, yet, the research on typical activities is quite limited. For example, there is not compelling evidence for the effectiveness of guidance curriculum activities. The focus of the research in school counseling tends to be on remedial activities. In terms of working with students with difficulties, there is some support for social skills training, family support programs, and peer counseling.

What are Characteristics of Effective School Counseling Programs?

Increasingly, the field of school counseling is moving toward providing services in a programmatic manner. School counselors no longer sit in their offices only counseling students in crisis. School counselors must implement a comprehensive program for all students that is a planned component of the larger school purpose and mission. There are very few studies, however, that have examined these comprehensive programs.

Wiggins and Moody (1987) compared the counseling programs of schools that were evaluated by students and a team of evaluators as being highly effective, average, or below average. This study found that counselors in the highly effective programs spent over 70% of their time in direct services (i.e., individual and group counseling activities) and very little time doing clerical activities. On the other hand, in school counseling programs that were rated as below average, the counselors spent between 24% to 43% of their time performing clerical tasks. Furthermore, the researchers found that the counselors who were spending a disproportionate part of their time performing clerical activities were not forced to do so by their administrators. The counselors in these below average schools did not have organized school counseling programs, nor were the majority of these counselors knowledgeable about implementing needs assessments and using such results for programmatic planning. Other research has found that parents, students, and teachers agreed that the least important activities for school counselors were paperwork, clerical tasks, and coordinating the testing program (Schmidt, 1995).

Hughey, Gysbers, and Starr (1993) surveyed students, parents, and teachers to determine if students served by a Missouri Comprehensive Guidance Program (MCGP) and patrons of the community were satisfied with the program. Even though school counseling is moving toward more classroom and group activities, the most frequent modality (72.9%) in which students reported interacting with counselors was individual sessions. Of the MCGP competencies areas (career planning and exploration, knowledge of self and others, and educational and vocational development), students rated the area of career planning and exploration as being the one in which counselors or teachers had helped them the most. These researchers found that one-fourth of the teachers believed counselors were involved in classroom guidance activities "a great deal," and 50% believed teachers were involved "some." In the area of group counseling, 20% thought the counselors were involved in this "a great deal," and 15% of the teachers were not aware that counselors performed any group counseling.

Schmidt (1995) described the process of external reviews of a school counseling program, and summarized the results of this review process with two school systems. Both of these school systems lacked well-defined kindergarten through Grade 12 school counseling programs. Without evidence of a defined program, it was difficult for either school system to clearly demonstrate the need for additional personnel. Although many school counselors may have developed well-defined school counseling programs at their individual schools, this trend is not reflected in the research (Whiston & Sexton, 1996). Developmental guidance programs are a dominate conceptual model for school counseling activities, but the research seems to focus on small components of this approach rather than on the comprehensive nature of its impact on a student body. We agree with Perry (1993), who concluded that if the trend toward comprehensive developmental guidance program is to continue, longitudinal programmatic research is needed to assess its value.

Integrating Research Into Practice: Conclusions and Implications

Given the state of current research we can suggest a number of conclusions. These conclusions are designed to facilitate the integration of research into school counseling practice.

1. Psychotherapy with children and adolescents has been found to be generally effective. The degree of effectiveness is similar to the effects of psychotherapy with adults. We do not know conclusively which specific factors influence outcome with children and adolescents. Tentatively, cognitive–behavioral interventions appear to be effective, but these techniques are more effective with older than with younger children. Behavioral interventions have also been supported in a number of studies. Relationship-based therapies do not seem to be as effective as either behavioral or cognitive–behavioral approaches. Parent training also seems to be an effective mode for intervening.

2. Previous outcome research in school counseling indicates that many activities performed by school counselors do indeed have a positive affect on students. Four meta-analytic studies have indicated that school counseling activities are moderately helpful to students using a variety of outcome measures. Reviews of outcome research in school counseling are generally positive about the effects of school counseling. Reviewers vary somewhat on the substantiveness of the current school counseling research.

3. School counselors need to be cautious in selecting activities, as not all of the activities investigated are supported by research. For example, at the elementary level, guidance curriculum activities designed to increase self-esteem did not necessarily increase self-esteem. Baker et al. (1984) found that programs that emphasized cognitive coping skills training, moral education, and substance abuse prevention, and that blended values clarification with other strategies were not very effective.

Research results do indicate, however, that individual planning interventions can have a positive impact on the development of students' career plans. Related to responsive services activities, there is some support for social skills training, family support programs, and peer counseling. Consultation activities have also been found to be an effective school counseling activity.

4. If we are to examine the totality of counseling outcome research, school counseling has the least amount of empirical evidence available to practitioners (Sexton, 1996). Relatively few outcome studies have been conducted to establish the effectiveness of school counseling activities. In addition, we found the overall quality

of the research studies deficient. Although there were some excellent studies, other studies had shoddy research methods and designs. For example, the outcome information provided by the researcher was sometimes as nebulous as one statement indicating the parents had reported that the program was beneficial. The majority of research in school counseling tends to be descriptive field studies, with only 22% of the studies incorporating an experimental design (Sexton, 1996). School counseling research needs to use methodologies used in other research areas, such as control groups, manualized interventions, and multiple outcome measures. It would also be helpful if more reviews of research were available. Journal editors may want to consider adopting the career counseling research model where annual reviews of research are published.

5. Whiston and Sexton (1996) found that the majority of the outcome studies in school counseling were related to remediation activities. They concluded that the large number of studies in this area might suggest that researchers, and potentially counselors, may be interested in remediating problems rather than focusing on developmental or preventative programs. We suggest that both researchers and counselors expand their attention to include preventative and developmental activities that may in the long run decrease the need for remediation. The philosophical core of school counseling is often touted to be preventative, yet it appears that the majority of research continues to be remedial in nature.

6. We encourage school counselors to become more actively involved in research activities. It is only through the active involvement of the school counselor in both consuming relevant research and participating in research activities that the quality and quantity of research-based knowledge will improve. The comparatively modest amount of research in this area may be problematic for the school counselor's role and responsibilities. For example, school counselors being assigned clerical duties may partly be due to our failure to conduct research and evaluation studies that clearly indicate that school counseling activities are necessary and beneficial to students. The last chapter in this book provides some practical methods for school counselors to implement outcome or evaluative studies. This may be a critical time for school counselors to produce

specific documentation concerning the positive effects that comprehensive and developmental school counseling programs have on children.

Our discussion of research-based school counseling activities concludes the second section of this book. These chapters have investigated the application of research findings to various setting in which counselors work. The following and final section of this book focuses on the integration of research and practice. Integrating research into practice means the practitioners must continually update their knowledge base. The next chapter describes efficient methods for accessing new research information. In the last chapter of the book, we present our model for the continued growth of the counseling knowledge base, which involves active participation by researchers, practitioners, and educators.

Integrating
Research
Into Practice

CHAPTER 7

Accessing and Using Counseling Research

If research and practice are to be truly integrated, counseling research outcomes need to be readily available to practitioners, and the day-to-day experiences of practitioners need to be readily available to researchers. In the past, this exchange of information was usually achieved only through special projects, conferences, seminars, and courses. Today, with the opportunity to search extensive databases on CD-ROM and to interact with other practitioners and researchers on the Internet, integrating practice and research is much more feasible.

Accessing Counseling Outcome Research

Until recently, accessing information about the outcomes of counseling research was time-consuming and either expensive or tedious. To request a reference librarian to conduct an online search from a commercial database vendor often meant waiting a week for the printout to arrive and, usually, paying a fairly hefty fee based on the number of citations requested. If the search results contained numerous irrelevant references (through miscommunication or lack of training and skill on the part of the searcher), the researcher's problems and frustrations were multiplied.

The alternative, to undertake the task by oneself, meant a trip to the library to manually search through numerous issues of print indexes such as *Psychological Abstracts, Education Index, Resources in Education (RIE)*, and the *Current Index to Journals in Education (CIJE)*. Even if the library provided CD-ROM access to ERIC, *PsychInfo*, and other databases, these self-service search stations became so popular that, in many university libraries, students and faculty alike have reported that they had to sign up as much as a month in advance to reserve a one-hour time slot.

Fortunately, in most university libraries, both turnaround time and expense to the individual have now dropped significantly. Still, these services are not readily available to practitioners outside academia. Moreover, the convenience of being able to acquire information either at home or in one's own office and the advantages of doing one's own searching, such as being able to experiment with various keywords, follow interesting leads (e.g., the works of a particular author), and limit the final output to only those references that are right on target, are very attractive. In this chapter, we will describe resources that provide researchers and practitioners alike the opportunity to conduct their own searches for information on counseling outcomes research and to obtain the information quickly and at a relatively low cost.

ERIC on CD-ROM

In general, CD-ROM subscriptions to the Educational Research and Information Clearinghouse (ERIC), *PsychLit, Social Work Abstracts, Family Studies*, and other databases are too expensive for individuals to purchase for their own personal use. Recently, however, the National Information Services Corporation (NISC) has produced a very inexpensive ERIC on CD-ROM product. For as little as $100 a year, subscribers can receive quarterly updates of the last 15 years of ERIC (including the full-text of over 1,000 ERIC *Digests*) in a highly user-friendly CD-ROM product. Three levels of search expertise are provided on each disc so that, as users become more skilled in searching, they can take advantage of more advanced strategies for refining their searches. At this time, the product is available for PCs only (i.e., there is no MAC version). For more information, contact the NISC at (410)

243-0797 or the ERIC Processing and Reference Facility at (301) 258-5500 or (800) 799-3742. The NISC disk is also described on the ERIC Facility's Web site at *http://www.ericfac.piccard.csc/nisc.html*.

Internet Resources for Accessing Information

The Internet offers seemingly endless opportunities to access research information and to interact with researchers and practitioners. Because the ERIC system is a federally funded program, its database and products are more readily available on the Internet than are the contents of databases such as *Psychological Abstracts*. However, the American Psychological Association's Web site, *http://www.apa.org/*, provides the user excellent leads to research-related resources such as electronic journals, online documents, bibliographies, and user groups. Of particular interest is their Psychcrawler, at *http://www.psychcrawler.com*, which is currently in the early stages of development, but appears to hold great promise for counselors and therapists seeking research information.

Electronic mail. Even the most basic use of Internet, electronic mail (e-mail), provides users with an opportunity to obtain very specific information about counseling research. AskERIC, a project begun in 1992, offers a personalized question-answering service using the resources of the entire ERIC system and beyond. By sending an e-mail message to *askeric@ericir.syr.edu*, individuals can receive a personal e-mail response within two business days. The response includes a list of citations relevant to the question as well as references to other Internet resources for additional information. Because most of the AskERIC questions dealing with any aspect of counseling are automatically forwarded to the information specialists at the ERIC Counseling and Student Services Clearinghouse (ERIC/CASS), users can also send their questions directly to the ERIC/CASS user services e-mail at *ericcas2@dewey.uncg.edu*.

Gopher and World Wide Web Sites. More than a dozen ERIC clearinghouses, adjunct clearinghouses, and support components host gopher and World Wide Web sites. For general information about ERIC and links to all ERIC Internet sites, users should start with the ERIC systemwide sites—gopher: *aspensys.aspensys.com:74/11/eric* or World Wide Web URL: *http://www.aspensys.com/eric2/welcome.html*. Several universities and other institutions also offer free public access to the ERIC database. A list of current public Internet access points to the ERIC database and step-by-step login instructions can be obtained by sending an e-mail message to *ericdb@aspensys.com*.

For complex database searching, we recommend the Web sites maintained by the ERIC Clearinghouse on Information and Technology, *http://eric.sunsite.syr.edu/*, and the ERIC Document Reproduction Service, *http://edrs.com/cgi-bin/askERIC*. The search engines at these Web sites offer complete Boolean logic searching (AND, OR, NOT) of a dozen citation fields.

Tips for Searching ERIC, Psychological Abstracts, PsychLIT, and PsychINFO

Although there may be hundreds or even thousands of documents and articles on any given topic, most users are interested in only a relatively small number of them. Limiting the search by specifying appropriate parameters helps locate desired resources without cumbersome trial-and-error efforts. The specific commands to use and procedures to follow will depend on the CD-ROM product or online service, but the following suggestions apply to all database searching.

1. Identify the major concepts of interest.

For example, the three major concepts addressed in research on developing children's social skills are: "research," "children," and "social skills."

2. Use the database's thesaurus (if available) to specify the descriptors.

Every document and article in ERIC and *Psychological Abstracts* is given subject indexing terms called *descriptors*. Descriptors for ERIC are listed, defined, and cross-referenced in the *Thesaurus of ERIC Descriptors*; information about descriptors for *Psychological Abstracts* is contained in the *Thesaurus of Psychological Index Terms*. To best capture a search topic, it is important to use the official descriptors most closely related. For example, in *Psychological*

Abstracts, items about the development of social skills would be indexed under the descriptor "*social skills;*" but, in ERIC, they would be indexed under the descriptor "*interpersonal competence.*"

3. Use Boolean logic to combine sets of descriptors.

Broadening or narrowing a search is achieved by placing the operators "AND," "OR," or "NOT" between sets of descriptors. AND narrows the search because the computer finds only those references that contain all terms listed. For example, "*children*" AND "*elementary school students*" would contain only those references that contain both terms. Conversely, OR would broaden the search because the computer would find all references that contain either children or elementary school students. The NOT operator should be used judiciously because it excludes references that contain multiple foci. For example, using "*counseling*" NOT "*therapy*" would exclude any reference that addressed counseling and therapy.

4. Use additional fields to further target the search.

Each record in ERIC and *Psychological Abstracts* contains at least a dozen fields such as title, author, publication date, publication type, geographic source, and so on. Obviously, searching by author or title helps immensely to locate a specific article or document, and limiting by publication year(s) can reduce a broad search to a more manageable size. One often overlooked field that can be very useful is the publication or document type. For example, if one is particularly interested in focusing on outcomes research, narrowing the search to include only Publication Type code 143 (Research/Technical Reports) would eliminate such things as opinion papers, classroom guides, program descriptions, and so on. For ERIC, a list of publication types and their codes can be found in the introduction to the Thesaurus.

Using Counseling Outcome Research

Accessing and acquiring information about counseling outcome research is an essential first step in integrating research and practice, but the critical factor is the extent to which individuals use the information to improve their practices and programs or to further their own research. Adapting one's thinking and practices to accommodate new information is not always easy; but, interacting with others with similar interests, questions, and concerns can help. Here again, the Internet offers unparalleled new opportunities for enhanced communication between and among researchers and practitioners.

Internet Resources for Enhancing Researcher/Practitioner Interaction

ListServs, mailing lists, UseNet groups, and chat rooms are all very popular online communication tools that can be used by those interested in enhancing how they can disseminate and use counseling outcomes research. Through these ways of online interactions, individuals can share their experiences or ask for advice on implementing a new program, solicit ideas for new and tried and true approaches to specific counseling problems, or learn about coming conferences and workshops. The openness of Internet-based discussions also allows for communication across disciplines, thus enriching the base of knowledge and experience. Because the number of potentially relevant groups is so large and changes rapidly, no attempt will be made here to identify them. Instead, we advise the reader to consult the home pages of various professional associations (e.g., American Counseling Association, American Psychological Association, National Association of School Psychologists, National Career Development Association, American School Counselor Association) for leads to current groups of interest.

To facilitate both intra- and interprofessional communication, ERIC/CASS has developed a collaborative network of professional association Web sites. The ERIC/CASS home page, *http://www.uncg.edu/~ericcas2,* is the base of the network, which offers a variety of information resources suited to a wide range of counseling specialty interests. Of special note are the "hot links" to the U.S. Department of Education Web site, and a variety of special services and resources supported by the U.S. Department of Education. A unique feature of the ERIC/CASS system is that it is linked with three other counseling association Web sites that ERIC/CASS assisted in developing and continue to support: the National Association of School Psychologists, National Career Development Association, and National Board of Certified Counselors. This arrangement not only facilitates communication and the sharing of ideas and resources among the members of each association, but also contributes to interactions between members across associations, such as, school counselors and school psychologists. This transfer of knowledge across disciplines helps make available the best practices from each discipline, and it encourages different types of specialists to teach and learn from one another. Additional organizations will be added to the network, but always on the condition that each organization must contribute as well as receive new ideas and resources.

New Directions in Information Resources

In addition to the increasing availability of electronic journals, three other special information resources have recently been developed that lend themselves to electronic communication and augment the information resources traditionally available to counseling professionals: digest collections, search collections, and integrated hard copy/CD-ROM products.

The ERIC/CASS digest collections offer 20–30 ERIC digests (papers of 1,500 to 2,000 words) on topics of high criticality, such as, counseling supervision, assessment in counseling and therapy, and research in counseling and therapy. Succinctly written and targeting the core substance of a topic, each digest requires only a fraction of the time needed to read longer articles and documents. Because of their ease of use and brevity, ERIC digests are the most popular of all ERIC publications and are available in full text both in the ERIC Digests Online (EDO) component of the ERIC database and on the ERIC/CASS Web site. A recent digest focused exclusively on research in counseling and therapy and could provide useful information to practitioners (Loesch & Vacc, 1977).

Treasure Chest II (Walz, Bleuer, & Bohall, 1996), another ERIC/CASS publication, is a step toward providing the user with a hard copy one-stop search collector covering topics of high interest to all of the helping specialties. Drawn from extensive online and CD-ROM searches of the ERIC database, *Treasure Chest II* provides annotations and abstracts of articles and documents on over 80 topics, with additional information provided through full-text copies of relevant ERIC digests.

Best Practices II is a unique resource developed by the National Association of School Psychologists. It consists of both a hard copy and a CD-ROM version of the same material; the CD-ROM version offers highly sophisticated searching capabilities so that the user can quickly locate, "bookmark," and even "highlight" particular sections of interest.

In this chapter, we have highlighted a few of the new directions that are emerging in the field of information dissemination and use. Through the use of the aforementioned CD-ROM products and Web sites, both practitioners and researchers can realistically continue their professional development and acquisition of new knowledge on an ongoing basis.

CHAPTER 8

Reconstructing the Research-Practice Relationship: Action Research in Clinical Practice

There has always been a relationship among the practice, research, and training activities of professional counseling. The case histories of the 1940s led to the theories of the 1950s. In turn, the outcome studies of the 1950s led to the proliferation of techniques and models of the 1960s and 1970s. The refined clinical findings concerning what works with whom was followed by the current stage of integrative approaches (Stricker, 1992). Although long-standing, this relationship is, however, a tenuous one. It is a relationship in which each pursues the same goals—effective counseling services—yet rarely speaks to the other. For example, consider the evidence that suggests the research-practice gap has grown to the extent that systematic research has little impact on practice.

As we progressed through this project, it became increasingly apparent to us that one of the major impediments to the integration of research into practice was the lack of an integrated model that united the activities of practice, research, and education. Even the scientist-practitioner models adopted by the American Psychological Association have not paved the way for integration. What is at stake here is the counselor's ability to provide the best counseling services to clients. Therefore, reconstructing the relationships between practice, research, and education is of the utmost importance for the counseling profession.

We argue that the relationship among practitioners, researchers, and educators needs to be a synergistic one. It needs to be based on the philosophy that all three activities are integral to the identity of professional counseling. As part of a synergistic relationship, practitioners would view research as a necessary clinical aid, educators would use models with empirical support as the basis of curricular decisions, and researchers would understand and inquire into relevant clinical questions. Moreover, if practitioners, educators and researchers work together, they will form a relationship in which they can collaborate to further strengthen the common knowledge base. We think that it is only when integrated relationships among these activities are forged that research will become a *regular* and unquestioned part of clinical decision making and practice will become the breeding ground for relevant research questions.

We have two goals in this final chapter. First, we propose an integrated model that we believe can serve as the basis of a reconstructed relationship among practice, research, and training. Our tripartite model illustrates how each contributes to the knowledge base in different ways and how each uses the knowledge base to accomplish different functions. As an extension of this proposed relationship, the second part of the chapter proposes a model of action research that might be used by practitioners to develop their own database for accountability and improvement. Finally, we conclude both the chapter and the book with some closing remarks.

Pragmatic Research Integration

One of the reasons a research-practice gap exists is because each of us has a tendency to view the world through our own "lens." Through our own lens, it is easy to see our activities as the most important. Consequently, it is no surprise that divisions between practice, research, and training have arisen. What gets lost in these myopic views is that practice, research, and training are mutually linked in two important ways. First, these activities share the same primary goal—effective and ethical services for clients. Second, although the specific duties of practice, research, and training differ, they are united by a mutual dependence on the same knowledge base.

We think that a reconstructed relationship among these activities needs to build on these two links—common purpose and shared knowledge. Furthermore, like Hoshmand and Martin (1995), we think that a synergistic relationship among practice, research, and training should be based on the principle of pragmatism. Pragmatic in the sense that the common goal of each is the solution of conceptual and clinical problems. As such, practice, research, and training would share the same motives—the best solutions to common problems. The best solutions are ones that work in furthering our knowledge and helping clients change. When sharing a common purpose based on pragmatism, no one of these activities drives the others. Instead, each makes a different, yet equally important contribution to effective counseling.

Figure 8.1 is our view of this synergistic relationship. We see practice, research, and education as the activities that collectively comprise professional counseling. Some counseling professionals are involved in one activity exclusively (e.g., practice), whereas other professional duties may include various activities (e.g., researcher and educator). In our model, all three of these activities are linked by their mutual dependence on a common knowledge base. To understand these relationships better, let us consider each element and the interaction among them.

Figure 8.1 *A Reconstructed Relationship between Research and Practice*

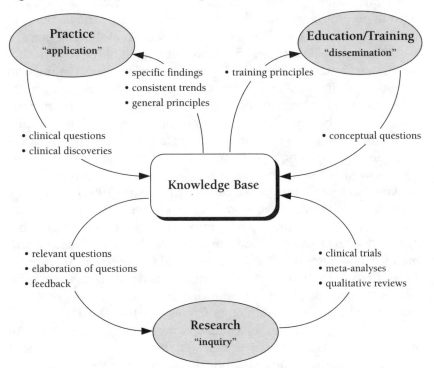

In our model, counseling **practice** is a pragmatic activity grounded in the evolving knowledge base that is derived from the broad range of scientific disciplines. As a pragmatic, problem-solving activity, the choice of interventions would depend on the particular client problem rather than on interventions that are commonly used or most preferred. Systematic research would be an integral part of clinical decision making. Because this knowledge base constantly evolves, clinicians would continually need to use it to remain informed.

We see the role of practice in this synergistic relationship as one that goes beyond the traditional received view, in which clinicians merely draw on science as the ultimate authority to solve client problems. Instead, the practitioner plays a crucial and unique role in enhancing the knowledge base in two important ways. First, practitioners are the ones in the trenches, who apply the knowledge base in clinical settings. The task of identifying pertinent and relevant questions falls to them. Second, we see the "practitioner" as a "local scientist" (Stricker & Trierweiler, 1995) who brings the skills of scientific inquiry to local phenomena. As such, they also use the methods of inquiry to evaluate their own effectiveness as action researchers, and in doing so develop a local database that might be used to promote and guide their individual practice. The methods of action research are the subject of the next section of this chapter.

Education is an often overlooked component of the relationship between research and practice. The goal of professional training is to develop and implement educational programs that prepare counselors to successfully help clients. Like researchers and practitioners, educators can become enmeshed in models that are more historically rooted than knowledge based. We propose that counselor educators also adopt a pragmatic stance. Training objectives become problems to be solved based on the use of our best and most current professional knowledge. Thus, as suggested by Peterson (1995), only those procedures with extensive research support would be taught. Furthermore, and sometimes more important, those procedures that repeatedly fail to show clinical use would not be part of training programs. Consequently, the curriculum would be based on the professional knowledge base, where empirical evidence dictates the models and techniques taught. As the knowledge base constantly evolves so must the curriculum of training programs (see Figure 8.1).

In this model, counselor education programs also need to train potential counselors to use research well. Research education should include the questions and methods unique to outcome research (see

Chapter 2). Counselors would be trained to perform empirically validated treatment approaches that fit particular clients. Furthermore, counselors would be taught action research methods so they can evaluate their own effectiveness. Counselors would leave their training program with the attitude that action research is an integral part of clinical decision making.

From our perspective, **research** should be viewed from a pragmatic standpoint, where it is seen as a problem-solving activity (Martin & Hoshmand, 1995). In the solution of problems, neither quantitative or qualitative research is primary. Instead, methodological choice is based on pragmatic goals realized through pluralistic methods. We agree with Stricker (1992)—different methodological processes just highlight different, not better, aspects of the data. Thus, determining whether a quantitative or qualitative method is needed depends on the problem being investigated and the questions that need answers (see Figure 8.1). Along this line, discovery-oriented questions would be matched with opened, qualitative investigations; confirmation and verification questions would use more traditional, quantitative questions. From our perspective, the questions researchers study cannot be determined in isolation. For, as we have said before, questions need to emanate from the activities of practice and education.

Beutler, Williams, Wakefield, and Entwistle (1995) suggested that the researcher may hold the key to reconstructing their relationship with practitioners. According to their recent survey, more practitioners are more interested in research than researchers may think. It is the academic researcher that does not acknowledge the value of clinical practice and thus, the burden of proof lies with the researcher to demonstrate that research findings are more relevant than experience (Beutler et al., 1995). Seligman (1996) suggested that researchers might be better able to integrate their activities with practitioners if they were to differentiate efficacy studies from those that measure efficiency. Efficacy studies are often associated with clinical research that involves clinical trials, has specific inclusion criteria for clients, and uses random assignment to highly specific treatments. Effectiveness questions focus on whether a treatment works in a clinical setting. Effectiveness research focuses on clinical usefulness and is thus specific to specific settings. The preferred method of addressing the question is a systematic, naturalistic design that emphasizes external validity and enhances the generalizability of findings to other clinical groups (Howard, Moras, Brill, Martinovich, & Lutz, 1996). Effectiveness research would involve not only measures of success but indications of cost effectiveness ratios. By focusing on effectiveness questions, researchers could better participate in the synergistic relationship suggested here.

The **knowledge base** that links these activities is an evolving one. Rather than providing definitive answers and ultimate truths, the knowledge base is constantly changing as new findings, interpretations, and questions are developed. Today's conclusions are quite naturally replaced by tomorrow's findings. In our field, the evolutional nature of knowledge is particularly evident. Some have suggested, for example, that the half-life of psychological knowledge is around 10 years (Kanfer, 1990). The implication is that the knowledge base must be a consistent and integral part of all facets of counseling—be it practice, research, or training.

The knowledge base for counseling is multifaceted and embodies an enormous amount of information. Information is continually infused into the knowledge base through a variety of sources such as theoretical monographs, professional organizations' statements and ethical standards, and conceptual articles. Each single research finding is, to some extent, incorporated into the knowledge base. Over time, common findings take the form of general principles—those findings that garner significant support over time and across varied clinical situations. In this book we presented a number of specific findings and general principles that make up the current knowledge base. Finally, through interpretation, these findings and principles become trends. It is important to remember that these trends are contextually dependent, and vary, like any interpretation, with professional, social, and personal issues of the time (see Figure 8.1).

The knowledge base also contains what we do not know—areas for which we have little systematic knowledge. These areas are holes in our understanding that are important because they generate new questions and future research efforts. Relevant and conceptually puzzling questions also become part of the knowledge base. They can arise from practitioners' attempts at applying theoretical models or from the discovery of new and potentially useful techniques. Like all parts of the knowledge base, relevant questions change over time as knowledge grows and interests change.

At any given time, the knowledge base has certain limitations, inadequacies, and inconsistencies. An awareness of these weaknesses is part of the climate of the knowledge base. Some of these limitations are due to inadequacies of method. In the first two chapters of this book, we outlined many of the current methodological problems inherent in the applied nature of counseling outcome research. The limitations of a knowledge base change. In some times, we strongly believe in our inquiry methods and are extremely confident in the validity and reliability of the principles and trends in what we know. At other times, our confidence in our approaches to inquiry wanes and the faith we place in the collective knowledge base decreases.

The mutual dependency of practitioners, researchers, and educators on the same **knowledge base** is fostered by the need for each to make use of the knowledge to perform their unique functions. Each, to some degree or another uses this knowledge to conduct its business. Stricker (1992) offered an expanded definition of *utilization* that illustrates its increasingly complex steps. The first, and simplest level, is that of awareness. Awareness is certainly the most common step of research utilization, but even it occurs less often that one would think in the current relationship between research and practice. The next step in using the knowledge base is actively considering the implications of the knowledge base. It is probably yet to be acted on, but at this level there is active thought about the role research would play in practice. Finally, the closest relationship is one in which the knowledge base is integrated in all aspects of clinical decision making. Ultimately, effective clinical decision making, relevant research, and professional training must rely on an integrated level of utilization.

In Figure 8.1 we attempt to demonstrate the manner in which these different components interact with one another. Practice, research, and education each draw on this knowledge base. In turn, each of these areas contributes to the knowledge base by forming hypotheses, asking relevant questions, and discovering new areas of interest. These questions become part of the knowledge base to be acted on by researchers. It is critical in this relationship that the knowledge base is viewed as an evolving one with strengths and limitations. For some questions research offers little guidance, whereas in other areas there is a wealth of relevant information. Even in those areas in which there are little or mixed research findings, research would still be the foundation of logical solutions to clinical problems. Thus, the question is never should research be integrated, but how.

Becoming an Action Researcher

For those primarily in the practitioner role, there may be advantages to incorporating research activities into daily duties. Practitioners are currently being asked to provide accountability information and documentation that the services they provide are effective. Clients, third-party payors, and school administrators are only a few of those who may want databased information concerning a counselor's effectiveness. Consequently, it may be to the counselor's advantage to not just be a research consumer but also a research producer. Examples of research that could be produced are an evaluation of a group for children whose parents have recently divorced, the percentage of a private practitioners' clientele who improve, an examination of the effects of a career exploration course on the drop-out rate of students, and whether involvement in individual counseling effects medical expenses.

Some counselors may view the research process as impersonal and remote, but others have actually suggested that the steps in designing a research study are similar to the steps in human service practice (Monette, Sullivan, & DeJong, 1990). Whiston (1996) proposed that there are analogous steps in counseling practice and outcome research as reflected in Table 8.1.

Identify the research question(s). Using Table 8.1 as a template, the first step in research is identifying the research question(s). This step is similar to the initial step in counseling—assessing the client's concern or problem. Identifying the research questions simply involves

Table 8.1 *Analogous Stages of Counseling Practice and the Research Process*

Stages in counseling	Stages in outcome research
Identifying problems or difficulties	Identifying research question(s)
Formulating goals	Formulating research design
Determining interventions	Determining measures of outcome and methods for ensuring treatment integrity
Implementing counseling	Collecting data
Appraising and evaluating progress	Analyzing data
Termination	Interpretation and conclusions

Note: From "Accountability through action research: Research methods for practitioners," by Susan C. Whiston, 1996, *Journal of Counseling and Development, 74,* pp. 616–623. Copyright 1996 by the American Counseling Association.

examining pertinent issues or problems in a counselor's work setting and forming these into one of the types of questions. In action research the question would be similar to those discussed in this book (Is it effective? What effects that efficacy? Can we enhance what has already been found to be effective?). Typical questions that may be asked by practitioners could be: Do the clients who participate in our services improve? Is a structured or unstructured group format more helpful with substance abuse clients? Could we improve our second-grade guidance curriculum by adding three more classroom sessions?

Formulate a research design. The second step in research is formulating the research design, a step that is analogous to formulating treatment goals, the second step in counseling (see Table 8.1). One's research questions, setting, and resources should guide the selection of the research design and methodologies. The purpose of any study is to attain well-founded conclusions, which cannot be drawn unless the action researcher carefully considers the design of the study. The methodologies and research designs discussed in Chapter 2 can aid an action researcher in designing an outcome study. Other useful resources on research designs are Heppner, Kivlighan, and Wampold (1993), Kazdin (1994), and Gelso (1979). For those interested in qualitative designs, Patton (1990) and Marshall and Rossman (1989) can be helpful references.

Ethical issues are a major consideration when designing a research study. The American Counseling Association *Code of Ethics and Standards of Practice* (ACA, 1995) contains specific ethical guidelines. Section G addresses ethical issues related to research in counseling. An often cited ethical dilemma concerns withholding treatment to have a control group. Some action research studies will randomly assign clients to a waiting list while the treatment is performed with the experimental group. This is not always a viable alternative in some counseling settings. Another alternative involves varying treatment, so that knowledge can be gained concerning which treatment is most effective with which clients. As an example, in career counseling some students would use the ABC computerized information system and another group would use the XYZ computerized system, with the results indicating which is more effective.

Determine methods for ensuring treatment integrity and measures of outcome. Methods for ensuring treatment integrity and the selection of outcome measures usually are considered part of formulating the research design; however, given the complexity of these topics in outcome research they will be addressed here as a separate step (see Table 8.1).

Treatment integrity is the extent to which the intended interventions or treatment is actually executed (see Chapter 2). A common sense approach to determining what treatment was provided would be to simply ask the counselors what they did in the sessions. However, a recent study (Wynne, Susman, Ries, Birringer, & Katz, 1994) indicated that therapists accurately recall only around 42% of the main session events immediately following the session. In addition, studies have found minimal associations among counselor, client, and nonparticipant observer perceptions of the same events (Caskey, Baker, & Elliot, 1984; Hill et al., 1988; Tichenor & Hill, 1989). Practitioners need to find practical methods for determining what interventions are being provided to draw conclusions about the effectiveness of those counselor actions. Iberg (1991) described a method of simply asking clients after the session the degree to which certain interventions were present.

The legitimate effect of a counseling intervention or approach cannot be determined without sound measures of client change. The selection of appropriate outcome measures is not an easy task. Studies have shown that the degree of outcome differs depending on whether the efficacy is judged by clients, counselors, or outside observers (Lambert, 1983; Orlinsky et al., 1994). The change process is complex and multidimensional making the assessment of counseling outcome a challenging and difficult undertaking. In terms of outcome measures, the old adage "more is better than less" seems to apply. According to Lambert and Hill (1994), the trends in outcome assessment are to (a) measure change from multiple perspectives (client, counselor, and outside observer), with several types of rating scales and methods; (b) use symptom-based and atheoretical measures; and (c) examine, as much as possible, patterns of change over time (see Chapter 2 for a more complete discussion).

Lambert, Ogles and Masters (1992) developed a conceptual scheme for categorizing outcome instruments so that practitioners and researchers can select instruments that generate data from a wide variety of viewpoints and domains (see Table 8.2). The first dimension is content, with the categories of intrapersonal (affect, behavior, and cognition), interpersonal, and social role. The second dimension is the source(s) of outcome information and includes the client self-report, counselor rating, trained observer, relevant other, or institutional sources categories. Common technologies or methods used to collect outcome data constitutes the third dimension, and they can be categorized into evaluation, description, observation, or status. The last category in Lambert et al.'s organization scheme (see Table 8.2) is time orientation and involves whether the instrument attempts a stable traitlike characteristic as opposed to an unstable, statelike characteristic. In selecting multiple outcome measures the goal is to gather comprehensive information; and this organizational scheme can assist researchers in selecting diverse methods of measuring outcome.

Data collection. After determining the outcome measures and the methods for ensuring treatment integrity, the next step is to collect the data (see Table 8.1). Cooperation of participating counselors and clients is critical in this step. A project can be enhanced by having the participating counselors involved in the research process early. If these counselors become invested during the planning stages they will be more likely to follow through with the often laborious task of data collection. Clients also will be more likely to complete the necessary paperwork or other data collection activities if they understand the purpose of a research project.

Table 8.2 *Classification Scheme for Outcome Measures*

Content	Source	Technology	Time Orientation
1. Intrapersonal Affect Behavior Cognition	1. Self-report	1. Evaluation	1. Trait
2. Interpersonal	2. Counselor rating	2. Description	2. State
3. Social role	3. Trained observer	3. Observation	
4. Relevant other	4. Status		
5. Institutional			

Note: From "Accountability through action research: Research methods for practitioners," by Susan C. Whiston, 1996, *Journal of Counseling and Development, 74,* pp. 616–623. Copyright 1996 by the American Counseling Association.

There are ethical considerations when clients or students are involved in collecting data. Particularly relevant to data collection are the ethical considerations of informed consent and confidentiality. Section G.2 in the *Code of Ethics and Standards of Practice* (ACA, 1995) is specifically devoted to issues related to informed consent. In addition, this ethical code states that "information obtained about research participants during the course of an investigation is confidential" (p. 38). This statement indicates that, in most instances, an individual's client data should not be accessible to the participating counselors. Numerous data collection difficulties can be avoided by attending to organizational details, such as thorough informed consent procedures, secluded space for completing outcome instruments, and methods for ensuring confidentiality.

Data analysis. After the data is collected, it must be analyzed. Some practitioners shy away from becoming involved with research because they view research as primarily being statistical analysis of some data. New statistical packages for the computer make data analysis simpler and more user friendly. In addition, if the design is qualitative, data analysis will involve nonquantitative methods. Qualitative designs often use descriptive methods for data analysis rather than standard statistical analyses. To accomplish this step it may be useful to consult a counselor educator, researcher, or statistician.

Interpret and draw conclusions. The final step within the process, interpreting the results, can be exciting. It is indeed gratifying to find that the majority of clients' symptoms decreased significantly, or that as a result of a 12-session classroom guidance program school children's self-esteem increased. Interpreting results is more complex than simply noting the statistically significant findings. Traditional statistical interpretation has been criticized because statistical significance does not guarantee that the results have clinical or practical meaning. Some researchers are proposing new methods for interpreting data in ways that more closely reflect clinical significance. Interpreting results of action research is grounded in the specific situation and what the results mean for the clients at that location. The results need to be carefully and objectively examined so that meaningful conclusions can be drawn. Some beginning researchers either over- or underinterpret results, and researchers must assess whether the conclusions they have drawn are merited by their results. The intent of many action research outcome studies is to evaluate current client services, and the results will often provide an indication of the quality of the services.

Outcome Methods in Specific Settings

The steps described here are applicable to outcome studies in a wide spectrum of counseling environments. The following expands on these methods and procedures and discusses performing outcome research in specific contextual settings.

Outcome Methods in Mental Health Counseling

As an example, let us consider a community counseling center that provides mental health services to individuals and specializes in the treatment of depression. This agency would like to have a contract for mental health services with a large managed care organization. This managed care organization wants information concerning the quality of the services provided by this community counseling agency.

Many agencies probably have some information existing in their files that can be used to begin to evaluate the efficacy of the services. It may be useful to simply calculate the percentage of clients who drop out or terminate prematurely; further analyses could explore differences between these two groups of clients. Some agencies have clients complete a satisfaction questionnaire after the last counseling session, that can serve as an initial outcome measure. Speer (1994) suggested that there are numerous benefits to community clinics initiating a pretreatment-posttreatment design, where a measure(s) would be easily assimilated into the admission and termination procedures of that agency. In the area of mental health counseling, commonly used outcome instruments are the Beck Depression Inventory (BDI), the State-Trait Anxiety Inventory (STAI), the Symptom Checklist-90 (SCL-90), and the Minnesota Multiphasic Personality Inventory (MMPI; Lambert & Hill, 1994). A listing of common outcome instruments in individual counseling is also listed in Sexton (1996). In gathering follow-up information, the outcome measures must be suitable for repeated measures and sensitive to durability and changes in outcome.

Another prominent method of assessing outcome is Goal Attainment Scaling (GAS; Kiresuk & Sherman, 1968), which was developed within a community mental health program. GAS requires that a number of mental health goals be formulated. For each specific goal, a scale with a graded series of likely outcomes is then specified. Outcomes range from *least* to *most favorable,* with not all goals receiving the same weight. The advantage of GAS is that it allows practitioners to evaluate treatment outcomes individually for each client, and provides counselors a concrete and systematic method of examining client change.

Using the categories in Table 8.2, we can demonstrate how the community counseling center could select outcome measures. One of the decisions the center would have to make is whether to use a gross rating of change or measure specific dimensions. If they want a gross rating, they might examine symptom reduction using the SCL-90. This could be useful information to provide to the managed care company because gross ratings of change generally result in larger effect sizes than ratings on a specific dimension or symptom (Lambert & Hill, 1994). Because it specializes in the treatment of depression, the community counseling center may want measures specifically related to depression. A commonly used instrument is the BDI. Using the categories in Table 8.2, we see that, as an instrument, the BDI's content is intrapersonal, its source is client self-report, its technology or method is descriptive, and it measures a client's current state of depression. Rather than using another client self-report instrument, a comprehensive method of evaluating this group would be to use the Hamilton Rating Scale for Depression (HRSD). The HRSD is another measure concerning current state, but is completed by clinicians. By way of illustration, if this agency decided to use only one measure, the BDI, their results may not compare favorably with a competing mental health agency that submits information using the HRSD. The HRSD has been found to produce a larger index of change than the BDI (Lambert, Hatch, Kingston, & Edwards, 1986). Thus, the community counseling agency, in this example, would have more sound information if they used multiple ratings of outcome.

Outcome Methods
in Career Counseling

As an example of action research related to career counseling, let us use a college counseling center that provides career counseling services to students. This college is experiencing some financial restraints and is looking at methods for saving money. The provost has suggested that a career counseling position should be cut from the counseling center to save funds. The college counseling center wants to show that the career groups this person facilitates are beneficial to the students.

In considering an outcome study, the action researcher needs to consider the group to be studied, the selection of appropriate interventions, and the methods for measuring outcome. Because of the developmental nature of career issues and selection, it is important that a career counseling researcher rule out the possibility that the positive change occurred simply as a result of the passage of time. Therefore, in career research it is often beneficial to use an experimental design that uses a control group. The college counseling center might consider randomly assigning students to a treatment group and a wait list control group. Those on the waiting list would receive career counseling after the treatment group had completed the career group.

In selecting outcome measures, counselors need to select ones that are not only appropriate measures for the interventions being studied but also appropriate for the clients' developmental stage (Herr & Cramer, 1992). As it is generally a good idea to use more than one measure, the counseling center may choose measures from the different categories of career outcomes. As noted in Chapter 5, the categories of career outcome measures are career decision making, effective role functioning, counseling evaluation, and miscellaneous. Sexton (1996) found that the most common outcome instruments used in career research are the *Career Decision Scale* (CDS), *Career Development Inventory* (CDI), *My Vocational Situation* (MVS), and *Survey of Career Development*. The CDS measures career decision-making skills, and the rest of these instruments would typically be considered measures of effective role functioning.

In the area of career decision making, the college counseling center could easily find out whether the level of career indecision significantly decreased as a consequence of participating in this career counseling group by using the CDS as a pre- and posttest. The CDS consists of only 19 items, and it gives a measure of both certainty and indecision and has strong psychometric qualities. Other examples of measures in this area are whether the students declared a major after completing the group or there was a decrease in the number of careers the students were considering.

The second prominent area of career outcome measures is effective role functioning, which includes both performance variables and adjustment variables. Examples of performance variables are academic performance and performance of skills (e.g., interviewing skills). The adjustment variables include measures of career maturity, self-concept change, locus of control, and cognitive complexity. Measures of career maturity are the most common outcome measure in this category (Oliver & Spokane, 1988; Whiston et al., 1996). However, there are several conceptual definitions of career maturity and various instruments that measure the construct (Betz, 1988). Frequently used instruments are the CDI and the Career Maturity Inventory (CMI). Career maturity measures are not conceptually appropriate for all clients, as they can be a valid measure for adolescence and college students but not for adults.

The third common area of career outcome measures concerns the evaluation of the counseling. Surprisingly, there does not appear to be any instruments that are consistently used in the research to examine satisfaction with, effectiveness of, or helpfulness of career counseling (Whiston & Sexton, 1995). A psychometrically sound career counseling evaluation instrument would be beneficial to both practitioners and researchers. Moreover, Oliver and Spokane (1988) have advocated for the development of a set of high quality criterion measures. Such a standardized set of instruments would greatly facilitate research related to career interventions and counseling.

Outcome Methods
in School Counseling

The example here is an elementary school counselor who has been doing some classroom guidance activities related to homework and study skills with fifth graders to assist them in making the transition into middle school.

There are some obstacles to performing counseling research in schools. Because of the increasing litigious environment in schools, many administrators are reluctant to approve innovative research projects. In addition, in school studies almost all of the research participants are minors, and as a result, informed consent requires parental consent. The logistics of obtaining parental consent are difficult, and some parents may be reluctant to allow participation if the study concerns emotional factors or gathers any information related to the home situation (Wilson, 1985). In this example, the counselors would need to have parental permission for the students to participate in the home work–study skills group and a separate permission form for them to participate in the research study.

Because of the guidance activity's focus on the transition from elementary to middle school, it might be helpful to examine measures typically used with both age groups. Gerler (1985), in his review of elementary school counseling research, lists outcome measures such as improved achievement scores, improved attendance, improved academic performance, improved behavior, and improved self-esteem. Concerning measures appropriate for middle school, St. Clair's (1989) review included outcome variables like referrals for disciplinary action, teacher report of disciplinary infractions, measures of self-concept or self-esteem, measures of achievement motivation, measures of sex-role stereotyping, and academic achievement.

Given the nature of this group, homework–study skills, it might be useful to see if there is any long-term effect related to the skills acquired. For example, it might be more useful to see if participation in the group effected the students' grades 1 year after completing the group rather than immediately after the group ended. School counselors should consider more follow-up assessments and longitudinal studies. These types of studies are particularly needed to determine the long-term effect of school counseling programs

Concluding Remarks

The preceding chapters have outlined what we believe to be a comprehensive overview of the current state of outcome research knowledge, as well as the issues related to the integration of research and practice. Throughout these pages, we argued that exclusive reliance on intuition and clinical experience is problematic. As an alternative, we propose that the integration of practice with research must become a priority for the counseling profession. That integration must, however, proceed with full knowledge of the limitations inherent in the applied nature of counseling outcome research. The integrated model we propose is not just based on research and practice, but also includes the critical element of education. It is a model in which research findings reach parity with other sources of information used in clinical decision making and curriculum development. From our perspective, we think this integration will happen when these three areas of professional counseling are seen as mutually dependent on one another, sharing a pragmatic focus on the common goal of effective counseling.

The chapters in the second section provided a compilation of current principles and trends, and described limitations that currently comprise the knowledge base of counseling. Many of these trends can be stable and could provide useful guidance for practice and education. Other findings need verification, thought, and further investigation. What is probably most difficult to accept is that some of these trends go against some of the cherished beliefs that have become part of the culture of counseling. If the field is to progress, it may be time to rethink some of these cherished notions.

Our investigations into outcome research has also led us to consider the future of outcome research in counseling. By far, the majority of studies presented here are quantitatively based studies of counseling efficacy. Although certainly useful, this body of knowledge suffers from a lack of discovery oriented studies. As we discussed in Chapter 2, including qualitative studies will provide a richness and detail that is needed in our search to understand counseling. In the long run, the addition of these types of investigations will go miles in overcoming the current research-practice gap.

Our hope is that if we were to revise this book in 5 years, we would find significant changes regarding the integration of research into counseling practice. First, we hope that the use of research in practice and education had become unquestioned—rendering many of the arguments for integration that we presented here irrelevant. We hope we would have to review an equal number of qualitative and quantitative studies; and we hope we would have more to say about the elements that comprise successful counseling and ways to further improve its efficacy. These hopes are not to say that we would expect the knowledge base to increase to the degree that it would be the primary source of guidance; instead, our hope is that systematic inquiry, whatever its method, would be central to the profession of counseling.

References

Alexander, J. F., & Luborsky, L. (1986). The Penn Helping Alliance Scales. In L. S. Greenberg & W. M. Pinsoff (Eds.), *The psychotherapeutic process* (pp. 325–366). New York: Guilford.

Allen, J. G., Deering, C. D., Buskirk, J. R., & Coyne, L. (1988). Assessment of therapeutic alliances in the psychiatric hospital milieu. *Psychiatry, 51*(3), 291–299.

American Counseling Association. (1995). *Code of ethics and standards of practice.* Alexandria, VA: Author.

American Psychiatric Association (1993a). Practice guidelines for eating disorders. *American Journal of Psychiatry, 150,* 792–794.

American Psychiatric Association (1993b). Practice guidelines for major depressive disorder in adults. *American Journal of Psychiatry, 150*(Suppl. 4). 1–26.

Anderson, E. M., & Lambert, M. J. (1995). Short-term dynamically oriented psychotherapy: A review and meta-analysis. *Clinical Psychology Review, 9,* 503–514.

Anderson, W. P., & Heppner, P. P. (1986). Counselor applications of research findings to practice: Learning to stay current. *Journal of Counseling and Development, 65,* 152–155.

Andrews, J. D. W. (1990). Interpersonal self-confirmation and challenge in psychotherapy. *Psychotherapy, 27,* 485–504.

Antonuccio, D. O., Davis, C., Lewinsohn, P. M., & Breckenridge, J. S. (1982). Identification of therapist differences in group treatment for depression. *Journal of Consulting and Clinical Psychology, 50,* 433–435.

Arbuthnot, J., & Gordon, D. A. (1986). Behavioral and cognitive effects of a moral reasoning development intervention for high-risk behavior-disordered adolescents. *Journal of Consulting and Clinical Psychology, 54,* 208–216.

Asay, T. P., Lambert, M. J., Christensen, E. R., & Beutler, L. E. (1984). *A meta-analysis of mental health treatment outcome.* Unpublished manuscript, Brigham Young University.

Atkinson, D. R. (1985). A meta-review of research on cross-cultural counseling and psychotherapy. *Journal of Multicultural Counseling and Development, 13*(4), 138–153.

Atkinson, D. R., Furlong, M. J., & Poston, W. C. (1986). Afro-American preferences for counselor characteristics. *Journal of Counseling Psychology, 33*(3), 326–330.

Atkinson, D. R., & Schein, S. (1986). Similarity in counseling. *The Counseling Psychologist, 14*(2), 319–354.

Auerbach, A. H., & Johnson, M. (1977). Research on the therapist's level of experience. In A. S. Gurman & A. M. Razin (Eds.), *Effective psychotherapy: A handbook of research* (pp. 84–102). New York: Pergamon Press.

Bachelor, A. (1988). How clients perceive therapist empathy: A content analysis of "received" empathy. *Psychotherapy, 25,* 227–240.

Bachelor, A. (1991). Comparison and relationship to outcome of diverse dimensions of the helping alliance as seen by client and therapist. *Psychotherapy, 28*(4), 534–549.

Baekland, F., & Lundwall, L. (1975). Dropping out of treatment: A critical review. *Psychological Bulletin, 82,* 738–783.

Baker, S. B., Swisher, J. D., Nadenichek, P. E., & Popowicz, C. L. (1984). Measured effects of primary prevention strategies. *Personnel and Guidance Journal, 62*(8), 459–464.

Bandura, A. (1986). *Social foundations of thought and action: A social cognitive theory.* Englewood Cliffs, NJ: Prentice Hall.

Barkham, M., & Shapiro, D. A. (1986). Counselor verbal response modes and experienced empathy. *Journal of Counseling Psychology, 33,* 3–10.

Barlow, D. H. (1981). On the relation of clinical research to clinical practice: Current issues, new directions. *Journal of Consulting and Clinical Psychology, 49,* 147–155.

Barlow, D. H. (1996). Health care policy, psychotherapy research, and the future of psychotherapy. *American Psychologist, 51,* 1050–1058.

Barlow, D. H., Craske, M. G., Cerney, J. A., & Klosko, J. S. (1989). Behavioral treatment of panic disorder. *Behavior Therapy, 20,* 261–282.

Barlow, D. H., O'Brien, G. T., & Last, C. G. (1984). Couples treatment of agoraphobia. *Behavior Therapy, 15*(1), 41–58.

Barrett-Lennard, G. T. (1962). Dimensions of therapist response as causal factors in therapeutic change. *Psychological Monographs, 76*(43, Whole No. 562).

Basoglu, M., Lax, T., Kasvcikis, Y., & Marks, I. M. (1988). Predictors of improvement in obsessive-compulsive disorder. *Journal of Anxiety Disorders, 2*, 299–317.

Bateson, G. (1972). *Steps to an ecology of mind.* New York: Ballantine Books.

Beck, A. T. (1988). *Love is never enough.* New York: Harper & Row.

Beck, A. T., & Emery, G. (1985). *Anxiety disorders and phobias: A cognitive perspective.* New York: Basic Books.

Beck, A. T., Sokol, L., Clark, D. A., Berchick, R., & Wright, F. (1992). A crossover study of focused cognitive therapy for panic disorder. *American Journal of Psychiatry, 149*(6), 778–783.

Bennun, I., & Schindler, L. (1988). Therapist and patient factors in the behavioural treatment of phobic patients. *British Journal of Clinical Psychology, 27*(2), 145–150.

Bergin, A. E. (1971). The evaluation of therapeutic outcomes. In A. E. Bergin & S. L. Garfield (Eds.), *Handbook of psychotherapy and behavior change* (pp. 217–270). New York: Wiley.

Bergin, A. E., & Garfield, S. L. (1971). *Handbook of psychotherapy and behavior change.* New York: Wiley.

Bergin, A. E., & Garfield, S. L. (Eds.). (1994). *Handbook of psychotherapy and behavior change* (4th ed.). New York: Wiley.

Bergin, A. E., & Lambert, M. J. (1978). The evaluation of therapeutic outcomes. In S. L. Garfield & A. E. Bergin (Eds.), *Handbook of psychotherapy and behavior change: An empirical analysis* (2nd ed., pp. 143–189). New York: Wiley.

Bergin, A. E., & Suinn, R. M. (1975). Individual psychotherapy and behavior therapy. *Annual Review of Psychology, 26*, 509–556.

Berman, J. S., & Norton, N. C. (1985). Does professional training make a therapist more effective? *Psychological Bulletin, 98*, 401–407.

Berzins, J. I. (1977). Therapist-patient matching. In A. S. Gurman & A. M. Razin (Eds.), *Effective psychotherapy. A handbook of research* (pp. 222–251). Oxford, England: Pergamon.

Betz, N. E. (1988). The assessment of career development and maturity. In W. B. Walsh & S. H. Osipow (Eds.), *Career decision making* (pp. 79–136). Hillsdale, NJ: Erlbaum.

Beutler, L. E. (1989). Differential treatment selection: The role of diagnosis in psychotherapy. *Psychotherapy, 26,* 271–281.

Beutler, L. E., & Bergin, J. (1991). Value change in counseling and psychotherapy: A search for scientific credibility. *Journal of Counseling Psychology, 38,* 16–24.

Beutler, L. E., & Clarkin, J. (1990). *Systematic treatment selection: Toward targeted therapeutic interventions.* New York: Brunner/Mazel..

Beutler, L. E., Consoli, A. J., & Williams, R. E. (1995). Integrative and eclectic therapies in practice. In B. Bongar & L. E. Beutler (Eds.), *Comprehensive textbook of psychotherapy* (pp. 274–292). New York: Oxford University Press.

Beutler, L. E., Crago, M., & Arizmendi, T. G., (1986). Research on therapist variables in psychotherapy. In S. L. Garfield & A. E. Bergin (Eds.), *Handbook of psychotherapy and behavior change* (pp. 257–310). New York: Wiley.

Beutler, L. E., Frank, M., Scheiber, S. C., Calvert, S., & Gaines, J. (1984). Comparative effects of group psychotherapies in a short-term inpatient setting: An experience with deterioration effects. *Psychiatry, 47*(1), 66–76.

Beutler, L. E., Machado, P. P. P., & Neufeldt, S. A. (1994). Therapist variables. In A. E. Bergin & S. L. Garfield (Eds.), *Handbook of psychotherapy and behavior change* (pp. 229–269). New York: Wiley.

Beutler, L. E., & Mitchell, R. (1981). Differential psychotherapy outcome among depressed and impulsive patients as a function of analytic and experiential treatment procedures. *Psychiatry, 44*(4), 297–306.

Beutler, L. E., Mohr, D. C., Grawe, K., Engle, D., & MacDonald, R. (1991). Looking for differential treatment effects: Cross-cultural predictors of differential psychotherapy efficacy. *Journal of Psychotherapy Integration, 1*(2), 121–141.

Beutler, L. E., Williams, R. E., Wakefield, P. J., & Entwistle, S. R. (1995). Bridging scientist and practitioner perspectives in clinical psychology. *American Psychologist, 50,* 984–994.

Bodden, J., & James, L. (1976). Influence of occupational information giving on cognitive complexity. *Journal of Counseling Psychology, 23,* 280–282.

Borders, L. D., & Drury, S. M. (1992). Comprehensive school counseling programs: A review for policymakers and practitioners. *Journal of Counseling and Development, 70*(4), 487–498.

Borokovec, T. D. (1991). *Progress report.* Unpublished grant proposal, Pennsylvania State University.

Boulougouris, J. C., Rabavilas, A. D., & Stefanis, C. (1977). Psychophysiological responses in obsessive-compulsive patients. *Behaviour Research and Therapy, 15*(3), 221–230.

Bouman, T. K., & Emmelkamp, P. M. G. (1993). *Panic disorder and severe agoraphobia: A comparative evaluation of exposure, breathing, retraining, and cognitive therapy.* Unpublished manuscript, University of Groningen, Germany.

Bowers, W. A. (1990). Treatment of depressed inpatients: Cognitive therapy plus medication, relaxation plus medication, and medication alone. *British Journal of Psychiatry, 156,* 73–78.

Braswell, L., Kendall, P. C., Braith, J., Carey, M. P., & Vye, C. S. (1985). "Involvement" in cognitive-behavioral therapy with children: Process and its relationship to outcome. *Cognitive Therapy & Research, 9,* 611–630.

Brown, J. (1987). A review of meta-analyses conducted on psychotherapy outcome research. *Clinical Psychology Review, 7*(1), 1–23.

Buckley, P., Karasu, T. B., & Charles, E. (1981). Psychotherapists view their personal therapy. *Psychotherapy: Theory, Research, and Practice, 18,* 299–305.

Burns, D. D., & Nolen-Hoeksema, S. (1991). Coping styles, homework compliance, and the effectiveness of cognitive-behavioral therapy. *Journal of Consulting and Clinical Psychology, 59*(2), 305–311.

Burns, L. E., Thorpe, G. L., & Cavallero, L. A. (1986). Agoraphobia 8 years after behavioral treatment: A follow-up study with interview, self-report, and behavioral data. *Behavior Therapy, 17*(5), 580–591.

Butler, G., Fennell, M., Robson, P., & Gelder, M. (1991). Comparison of behavior therapy and cognitive behavior therapy in the treatment of generalized anxiety disorder. *Journal of Consulting and Clinical Psychology, 59,* 167–175.

Calsyn, R. J., & Davidson, W. S. (1978). Do we really want a program evaluation strategy based solely on individualized goals? A critique of goal attainment scaling. *Community Mental Health Journal, 14*(4), 300–308.

Calvert, S. J., Beutler, L. E., & Crago, M. (1988). Psychotherapy outcome as a function of therapist-patient matching on selected variables. *Journal of Social and Clinical Psychology, 6*(1), 104–117.

Casey, R. J., & Berman, J. S. (1985). The outcome of psychotherapy with children. *Psychological Bulletin, 98*(2), 388–400.

Caskey, N., Baker, C., & Elliott, R. (1984). Dual perspectives: Clients' and therapists' perceptions of therapists' responses. *British Journal of Clinical Psychology, 23*, 30–40.

Cherbosque, J. (1987). Differential effects of counselor self-disclosure statements on perception of the counselor and willingness to disclose: A cross-cultural study. *Psychotherapy, 24*, 434–437.

Christensen, H., Hadzi-Pavlovic, D., Andrews, G., & Mattick, R. (1987). Behavior therapy and tricyclic medication in the treatment of obsessive-compulsive disorder: A quantitative review [Special issue: Eating disorders]. *Journal of Consulting and Clinical Psychology, 55*(5), 701–711.

Christenson, A., & Jacobson, N. S. (1993). Who (or what) can do psychotherapy: The status and challenge of nonprofessional therapies. *Psychological Science, 5*(1), 8–14.

Ciechalski, J. C., & Schmidt, M. W. (1995). The effects of social skills training on students with exceptionalities. *Elementary School Guidance and Counseling, 29*, 217–222.

Claiborn, C. D., & Lictenberg, J. W. (1989). Interactional counseling. *The Counseling Psychologist, 17*, 355–453.

Clark, D. M. (1986). A cognitive approach to panic. *Behavior Research and Therapy, 24*, 461–470.

Clark, D. M. (1991, September). *Cognitive therapy for panic disorder.* Paper presented at the National Institutes of Health Consensus Development Conference on Treatment of Panic Disorder, Washington, DC..

Clark, D. M., Salkovskis, P. M., Hackmann, A., Middleton, H., & Gelder, M. (1992). *A comparison of cognitive therapy, applied relaxation and inipramine in the treatment of panic disorder.* Manuscript submitted for publication.

Clarkin, J. F., Glick, I. D., Haas, G., & Spencer, J. H. (1991). The effects of inpatient family intervention on treatment outcome. In S. M. Mirin, S. T. Gossett, & M. C. Grob (Eds.), *Psychiatric treatment: Advances in outcome research* (pp. 47–59). Washington, DC: American Psychiatric Association.

Clemental-Jones, C., Malan, D., & Trauer, T. (1990). A retrospective follow-up study of 84 patients treated with individual psychoanalytic psychotherapy: Outcome and predictive factors. *British Journal of Psychotherapy, 6*(4), 363–374.

Clum, G. A. (1989). Psychological interventions vs. drugs in the treatment of panic. *Behavior Therapy, 20*(3), 429–457.

Coady, N. F. (1991). The association between complex types of therapist interventions and outcomes in psychodynamic psychotherapy. *Research on Social Work Practice, 1*(3), 257–277.

Cohen, J. (1977). *Statistical power analysis for the behavioral sciences.* New York: Academic Press.

Cohen, J. (1988). *Statistical power analysis for the behavioral scienes* (2nd ed.). Hillsdale, NJ: Erlbaum.

Cohen, L. H., Sargent, M. M., & Sechrest, L. B. (1986). Use of psychotherapy research by professional psychologists [Special issue: Psychotherapy research]. *American Psychologist, 41*(2), 198–206.

Connolly, M. B., & Strupp, H. H. (1996). Cluster analysis of patient reported psychotherapy outcomes. *Psychotherapy Research, 6,* 16–29.

Consumer Reports (1995, November). Mental health: Does therapy help? 734–739.

Cooper, H. M. (1982). Scientific guidelines for conducting integrative research reviews. *Review of Educational Research, 52*(2), 291–302.

Costell, E. J. (1989). Developments in child psychiatric epidemiology. *Journal of the American Academy of Child and Adolescent Psychiatry, 28,* 836–841.

Crites, J. O. (1981). *Career counseling.* New York: McGraw-Hill.

Crits-Christoph, P. (1992). The efficacy of brief dynamic psychotherapy: A meta-analysis. *American Journal of Psychiatry, 149*(2), 151–158.

Crits-Christoph, P., Baranackie, K., Kurcias, J. S., Beck, A. T., Carroll, K., Perry, K., Luborsky, L., McLellan, A. T., Woody, G. E., Thompson, L., Gallagher, D., & Zitrin, C. (1991). Meta-analysis of therapist effects in psychotherapy outcome studies. *Psychotherapy Research, 1*(2), 81–91.

Crits-Christoph, P., Cooper, A., & Luborsky, L. (1988). The accuracy of therapists' interpretations and the outcome of dynamic psychotherapy. *Journal of Consulting and Clinical Psychology, 56*(4), 490–495.

Crits-Christoph, P., & Mintz, J. (1991). Implications of therapist effects for the design and analysis of comparative studies of psychotherapies. *Journal of Consulting and Clinical Psychology, 59*(1), 20–26.

Cronbach, L. M. (1975). Dissent from Craver. *American Psychologist, 30,* 602–603.

Dawes, R. M. (1979). The robust beauty of improper linear models in decision making. *American Psychologist, 34,* 571–582.

Dawes, R. M. (1986). Representational thinking in clinical judgement [Special issue: Personality assessment in the 80s: Issues and advances]. *Clinical Psychology Review, 6*(5), 425–441.

Dawes, R. M. (1991). Hypothetical studies and civil liberties. *American Psychologist, 46,* 882.

Dawes, R. M. (1994). *House of cards: Psychology and psychotherapy built on myth.* New York: Free Press

Dawes, R. M., Faust, D., & Meehl, P. E. (1989). Clinical versus artuarial judgement. *Science, 243,* 1668–1674.

DeRubeis, R. J., Evans, M. D., Hollins, S. D., Garvey, M. J., Grove, W. M., & Tuason, V. B. (1990). How does cognitive therapy work? Cognitive change and symptom change in cognitive therapy and pharmacotherapy for depression. *Journal of Consulting and Clinical Psychology, 58,* 862–869.

DeRubeis, R. J., & Feeley, M. (1990). Determinants of change in cognitive therapy for depression. *Cognitive Therapy and Research, 14*(5), 469–482.

Dobson, K. S. (1989). A meta-analysis of the efficacy of cognitive therapy for depression. *Journal of Consulting and Clinical Psychology, 57*(3), 414–419.

Dodd, J. A. (1970). A retrospective analysis of variables related to duration of treatment in a university psychiatric clinic. *Journal of Nervous and Mental Disease, 151,* 75–85.

Donley, R. J., Horan, J. J., & DeShong, R. L. (1989). The effect of several self-disclosure permutations on counseling process and outcome. *Journal of Counseling and Development, 67*(7), 408–412.

Dorn, F. J. (1989). An examination of client motivation and career certainty. *Journal of College Student Development, 30,* 237–241.

Duan, C., & Hill, C. E. (1996). The current state of empathy research. *Journal of Counseling Psychology 43,* 261–274.

DuBrin, J. R., & Zastowny, T. R. (1988). Predicting early attrition from psychotherapy: An analysis of a large private-practice cohort [Special issue: Psychotherapy and the new health care systems]. *Psychotherapy, 25*(3), 393–408.

Dunn, C. W., & Veltman, G. C. (1989). Addressing the restrictive career maturity patterns of minority youth: A program evaluation. *Journal of Multicultural Counseling and Development, 17*(4), 156–164.

Durlak, J. A. (1980). Comparative effectiveness of behavioral and relationship group treatment in the secondary prevention of maladjustment. *American Journal of Community Psychology, 8*, 327–339.

Durlak, J. A., Fuhrman, T., & Lampman, C. (1991). Effectiveness of cognitive-behavior therapy for maladapting children: A meta-analysis. *Psychological Bulletin, 110*(2), 204–214.

Dush, D. M., Hirt, M. L., & Schroeder, H. E. (1983). Self-statement modification with adults: A meta-analysis. *Psychological Bulletin, 94*(3), 408-422.

Eden, D., & Avriam, A. (1993). Self-efficacy to speed reemployment: Helping people to help themselves. *Journal of Counseling Psychology, 78*, 352–360.

Eisenthal, S., Emery, R., Lazare, A., & Udin, H. (1979). "Adherence" and the negotiated approach to patienthood. *Archives of General Psychiatry, 36*, 393–398.

Elkin, I., Shea, M. T., Watkins, J. T., Imber, S. D., Sotsky, S. M., Collins, J. F., Glass, D. R., Pilkonis, P. A., Leber, W. R., Docherty, J. P., Fiester, S. J., & Parloss, M. B. (1989). National Institute of Mental Health Treatment of Depression Collaborative Research Program: General effectiveness of treatments. *Archives of General Psychiatry, 46*(11), 971–982.

Elliott, R., Baker, C. B., Caskey, N., & Pistrange, N. (1982). Differential helpfulness of counselor verbal response modes. *Journal of Counseling Psychology, 29*(4), 354–361.

Elliott, R., Clark, C., Wexler, M., Kemeny, V., Brinkerhoff, J., & Mack, C. (1990). The impact of experiential therapy of depression: Initial results. In G. Lietaer, J. Rombauts, & R. Van Balen (Eds.), *Client-centered and experiential psychotherapy in the nineties* (pp. 549–577). Leuven, Belgium: Leuven University Press.

Ellis, M. V. (1991). Conducting and reporting integrative research reviews: Accumulating scientific knowledge. *Counselor Education and Supervision, 30*, 225–237.

Emmelkamp, P. M. G. (1980). Agoraphobics' interpersonal problems: Their role in the effects of exposure in vivo therapy. *Archives of General Psychiatry, 37*, 1303–1306.

Emmelkamp, P. M. G. (1994). Behavior therapy with adults. In A. E. Bergin & S. L. Garfield (Eds.), *Handbook of psychotherapy and behavior change* (pp. 379–427). New York: Wiley.

Emmelkamp, P. M. G., & Beens, H. (1991). Cognitive therapy with obsessive-compulsive disorder: A comparative evaluation. *Behaviour Research and Therapy, 29*(3), 293–300.

Emmelkamp, P. M. G., Brilman, E., Kuipers, H., & Mersch, P. P. (1986). The treatment of agoraphobia: A comparison of self-instructional training, rational emotive therapy, and exposure in vivo. *Behavior Modification, 10*(1), 37–53.

Emmelkamp, P. M. G., Mersch, P. P., Vissia, E., & Van-der-Helm, M. (1985). Social phobia: A comparative evaluation of cognitive and behavioral interventions. *Behaviour Research and Therapy, 23*(3), 365–369.

Emmelkamp, P. M. G., & Scholing, A. (1990). Behavioral treatment for simple and social phobics. In G. D. Burrows, R. Noyes, & G. M. Roth (Eds.), *Handbook of anxiety* (Vol. 4, pp. 327–361). Amsterdam: Elsevier.

Emmelkamp, P. M. G., van Linden van den Heuvell, G., Ruphan, M., & Sanderman, R. (1989). Home-based treatment of obsessive-compulsive patients: Intersession interval and therapist involvement. *Behaviour Research and Therapy, 27*, 89–93.

Emmelkamp, P. M. G., Visser, S., & Hoekstra, R. J. (1988). Cognitive therapy vs exposure in vivo in the treatment of obsesssive-compulsives. *Cognitive Therapy and Research, 12*, 103–144.

Emmelkamp, P. M. G., & Wessels, H. (1975). Flooding in imagination vs. flooding in vivo: A comparison with agoraphobics. *Behaviour Research and Therapy, 13*, 7–16.

Eysenck, H. J. (1952). The effects of psychotherapy: An evaluation. *Journal of Consulting Psychology, 16*, 319–324.

Falvey, E. (1989). Passion and professionalism: Critical rapprochement for mental health research. *Journal of Mental Health Counseling, 11*, 86–95.

Foa, E. B., Steketee, G. S., Grayson, J. B., Turner, R. M., & Latimer, P. R. (1984). Deliberate exposure and blocking of obsessive-compulsive rituals: Immediate and long term effects. *Behavior Therapy, 15*, 450-472.

Fonagy, P., & Target, M. (1994). The efficacy of psychoanalysis for children with disruptive disorders. *Journal of the American Academy of Child and Adolescent Psychiatry, 33*, 45–55.

Forehand, R., & Long, N. (1988). Outpatient treatment of the acting out child: Procedures, long-term follow-up data, and clinical problems. *Advances in Behaviour Research and Therapy, 10,* 129–177.

Francis, J. R., & Aronson, H. (1990). Communicative efficacy of psychotherapy research. *Journal of Consulting and Clinical Psychology, 58,* 368–370.

Frank, A. F., & Gunderson, J. G. (1990). The role of the therapeutic alliance in the treatment of schizophrenia: Relationship to course and outcome. *Archives of General Psychiatry, 47*(3), 228–236.

Frank, E., Kupfer, D. J., & Perel, J. M. (1989). Early recurrence in unipolar depression. *Archives of General Psychiatry, 46*(5), 397–400.

Frank, J. D. (1959). The dynamics of the psychotherapeutic relationship. *Psychiatry, 22,* 17–39.

Frank, J. D. (1971). Therapeutic factors in psychotherapy. *American Journal of Psychotherapy, 25,* 350-361.

Frank, J. D. (1976). Psychotherapy and the sense of mastery. In R. L. Spitzer & D. F. Klein (Eds.), *Evaluation of psychotherapies: Behavioral therapies, drug therapies and their interactions* (pp. 47–56). Baltimore: The Johns Hopkins University Press.

Fretz, B. R. (1981). Evaluating the effectiveness of career interventions. *Journal of Counseling Psychology, 18,* 77–90.

Friedlander, M. L., Thibodeau, J. R., & Ward, L. G. (1985). Discriminating the "good" from the "bad" therapy hour: A study of dyadic interaction. *Psychotherapy, 22,* 631–642.

Friedman, H. J. (1963). Patient-expectancy and symptom reduction. *Archives of General Psychiatry, 8,* 61–67.

Froyd, J., & Lambert, M. J. (1989, May). *A survey of outcome research measures in psychotherapy research.* Paper presented at the meeting of the Western Psychological Association, Reno, NV.

Galassi, J. P., Crace, R. K., Martin, G. A., James, R. M., Jr., & Wallace, R. L. (1992). Client preferences and anticipations in career counseling: A preliminary investigation. *Journal of Counseling Psychology, 39,* 46–55.

Gallagher-Thompson, D., Hanley-Peterson, P., & Thompson, L. W. (1990). Maintenance of gains versus relapse following brief psychotherapy for depression. *Journal of Consulting and Clinical Psychology, 58*(3), 371–374.

Garfield, S. L. (1986). Research on client variables in psychotherapy. In S. L. Garfield & A. E. Bergin (Eds.), *Handbook of psychotherapy and behavior change* (pp. 213–256). New York: Wiley.

Garfield, S. L. (1994). Research on client variables in psychotherapy. In A. E. Bergin & S. L. Garfield (Eds.), *Handbook of psychotherapy and behavior change* (pp. 190–228). New York: Wiley.

Garfield, S. L., & Bergin, A. E. (1971). Therapeutic conditions and outcome. *Journal of Abnormal Psychology, 77,* 108–114.

Garfield, S. L., & Bergin, A. E. (1986). Introduction and historical overview. In S. L. Garfield & A. E. Bergin (Eds.), *Handbook of psychotherapy and behavioral change* (pp. 3–22). New York: Wiley.

Garis, J. W., & Niles, S. G. (1990). The separate and combined effects of SIGI and DISCOVER and a career planning course on undecided university students. *Career Development Quarterly, 39,* 261–274.

Gelernter, C. S., Uhde, T. W., Cimbolic, P., Arnkoff, D. B., Vittone, B. J., Tancer, M. E., & Bartko, J. J. (1991). Cognitive-behavioral and pharmacological treatments of social phobia: A controlled study. *Archives of General Psychiatry, 48*(10), 938–945.

Gelso, C. J. (1979). Research in counseling: Methodological and professional issues. *The Counseling Psychologist, 8*(3), 7–36.

Gerler, E. R. (1985). Elementary school counseling research and the classroom learning environment. *Elementary School Guidance & Counseling, 20,* 39–40.

Gerler, J. D. (1984). The imagery in BASIC ID: A factor in education. *Journal of Humanistic Education and Development, 22,* 115–122.

Goldfield, M. R., Greenberg, L. S., & Marhar, C. (1990). Individual psychotherapy: Process and outcome. *Annual Review of Psychology, 41,* 659–688.

Goldfried, M. R., & Wolfe, B. E. (1996). Psychotherapy practice and research: Repairing a strained alliance. *American Psychologist, 51,* 1007–1016.

Goldstein, A. P. (1960). Patients' expectancies and nonspecific therapy as a basis for (un)spontaneous remission. *Journal of Clinical Psychology, 16,* 399–403.

Goldstein, J. M., Cohen, P., Lewis, S. A., & Struening, E. L. (1988). Community treatment environments: Patient vs. staff evaluations. *Journal of Nervous and Mental Disease, 176,* 227–233.

Grawe, K. (1989). Von der psychotherapeutischen outcome - Forschung zur differentiellen Prozessanalyse [From psychotherapeutic outcome research to differential process analysis]. *Zeitschrift-fur-Klinische-Psychologie. Forschung und Praxis, 18*(1), 23–34.

Grawe, K., Caspar, F., & Ambuhl, H. (1990). Differentielle Psychotherapieforschung: Vier Therapieformen im Vergleich [Topical issue: Differential psychotherapy research: Comparative evaluation of four forms of therapy]. *Zeitschrift fur Klinische Psychologie, 19,* 287–376.

Green, B. C., Gleser, G. C., Stone, W. N., & Siefert, R. F. (1975). Relationship among diverse measures of psychotherapy outcome. *Journal of Consulting and Clinical Psychiatry, 43,* 689–699.

Greenberg, L. S., Elliott, R. K., & Lietaer, G. (1994). Research on experiential psychotherapies. In A. E. Bergin & S. L. Garfield (Eds.), *Handbook of psychotherapy and behavior change* (pp. 509–539). New York: Wiley.

Greenberg, L. S., Rice, L. N., & Elliott, R. (1993). *Process-experiential therapy: Facilitating emotional change.* New York: Guilford.

Greenberg, R. P., & Stalker, J. (1981). Personal therapy for therapists. *American Journal of Psychiatry, 138,* 1467–1471.

Gurin, G., Veroff, J., & Feld, S. (1960). Americans view of their mental health. (Joint Commission on Mental Illness and Health, Monograph Series No. 4). New York: Basic Books.

Gurman, A. S. (1977). The patient's perceptions of the therapeutic relationship. In A. S. Gurman & A. M. Razin (Eds.), *Effective Psychotherapy* (pp. 503–545). New York: Pergamon Press.

Gurman, A. S., & Kniskern, D. P. (1978). Research on marital and family therapy: Progress, perspective, and prospect. In S. L. Garfield & A. E. Bergin (Eds.), *Handbook of psychotherapy and behavior change: An empirical analysis* (2nd ed., pp. 817–901). New York: Wiley.

Gurman, A. S., & Kniskern, D. P. (1986). Research on marital and family therapies. In S. L. Garfield & A. E. Bergin (Eds.), *Handbook of psychotherapy and behavior change* (3rd ed., pp. 565–624). New York: Wiley.

Gysbers, N. C., & Henderson, P. (1994). *Developing and managing your school guidance program.* Alexandria, VA: American Counseling Association.

Hackett, G. (1993). Career counseling and psychotherapy: False dichotomies and remended remedies. *Journal of Career Assessment, 1,* 105–117.

Hadley, H. R. (1988). Improving reading scores through a self-esteem intervention program. *Elementary School Guidance and Counseling, 22*(3), 248–252.

Hagborg, W. J. (1993). Middle-school student satisfaction with group counseling: An initial study. *Journal for Specialists in Group Work, 18*(2), 80–85.

Heimberg, R. G., Dodge, C. S., Hope, D. A., Kennedy, C. R., Zollo, L. J., & Becker, R. E. (1990). Cognitive behavioural group treatment for social phobias: A comparison with a credible placebo control. *Cognitive Therapy and Research, 14,* 1–23.

Henry, W. P. (1990, June). *The use of the SASB INTREX questionnaire to measure change in cyclical maladaptive interpersonal patterns.* Symposium presented at the annual meeting of the Society for Psychotherapy Research, Wintergreen, VA.

Henry, W. P., Bardo, H. R., & Henry, C. A. (1992). The effectiveness of career development seminars on African American premedical studies. *Journal of Multicultural Counseling and Development, 20*(3), 99-112.

Henry, W. P., Schacht, T. E., & Strupp, H. H. (1986). Structural analysis of social behavior: Application to a study of interpersonal process in differential psychotherapeutic outcome [Special issue: Psychotherapy research]. *Journal of Consulting and Clinical Psychology, 54*(1), 27–31.

Henry, W. P., Schacht, T. E., & Strupp, H. H. (1990). Patient and therapist introject, interpersonal process, and differential psychotherapy outcome. *Journal of Consulting and Clinical Psychology, 58*(6), 768–774.

Henry, W. P., Strupp, H. H., Butler, S. F., Schacht, T. E., & Binder, J. L. (1993). The effects of training in time-limited dynamic psychotherapy: Changes in therapist behavior. *Journal of Consulting and Clinical Psychology, 61,* 434–440.

Henry, W. P., Strupp, H. H., Schacht, T. E., & Gaston, L. (1994). Psychodynamic approaches. In A. E. Bergin & S. L. Garfield (Eds.), *Handbook of psychotherapy and behavior change* (pp. 467–508). New York: Wiley.

Heppner, P. P., & Claiborn, C. D. (1989). Social influence research in counseling: A review and critique. *Journal of Counseling Psychology, 36,* 365–387.

Heppner, P. P., Kivlighan, D. M., Jr., & Wampold, B. E. (1993). *Research design in counseling.* Pacific Grove, CA: Brooks/Cole.

Herr, E. L., & Cramer, S. H. (1992). *Career guidance and counseling through the life span: Systematic approaches* (4th ed.). New York: HarperCollins.

Herr, E. L., & Cramer, S. H. (1996). *Career guidance and counseling through the life span: Systematic approaches* (5th ed.). New York: HarperCollins.

Highlen, P. S., & Hill, C. E. (1984). Factors affecting client change in individual counseling: Current status and theoretical speculations. In S. D. Brown & R. W. Lent (Eds.), *Handbook of counseling psychology* (pp. 334-396). New York: Wiley.

Hill, C. E. (1982). Counseling process research: Philosophical and methodological dilemmas. *The Counseling Psychologist, 10*(4), 7–19.

Hill, C. E., Helms, J. E., Tichenor, V., Speigel, S. B., O'Grady, K. E., & Perry, E. (1988). Effects of therapist response modes in brief psychotherapy. *Journal of Counseling Psychology, 35*(3), 222–233.

Hill, C. E., Nutt, E. A., & Jackson, S. (1994). Trends in psychotherapy process research: Samples, measures, researchers, and classic publications. *Journal of Counseling Psychology, 41,* 364–377.

Hill, K. A. (1987). Meta-analysis of paradoxical interventions. *Psychotherapy, 24*(2), 266–270.

Holland, J. L., Magoon, T. M., & Spokane, A. R. (1981). Counseling psychology: Career interventions, research, and theory. *Annual Review of Psychology, 32,* 279-305.

Hollon, S. D., Shelton, R. C., & Loosen, P. T. (1991). Cognitive therapy and pharmacotherapy for depression. *Journal of Consulting and Clinical Psychology, 59,* 88–99.

Holloway, E. L., & Wampold, B. E. (1986). Relation between conceptual level and counseling-related tasks: A meta-analysis. *Journal of Counseling Psychology, 33,* 310–319.

Hoogduin, C. A. L., Duivenvoorden, H., Schapap, C., & de Haan, E. (1989). On the outpatient treatment of obsessive-compulsives: Outcome, prediction of outcome and follow-up. In P. M. G. Emmelkamp, E. T. A. M. Everaerd, F. Kraaimaat, & M. van Son (Eds.), *Fresh perspectives on anxiety disorders.* Amsterdam: Swets.

Horowitz, M. J., Marmar, C., Weiss, D. S., DeWitt, K. N., & Rosenbaum, R. (1984). Brief psychotherapy of bereavement reactions: The relationship of process to outcome. *Archives of General Psychiatry, 41,* 438–448.

Horvath, A. O., & Greenberg, L. S. (1986). The development of the Working Alliance Inventory. In L. S. Greenberg & W. M. Pinsoff (Eds.), *The psychotherapeutic process: A research handbook* (pp. 529–556). New York: Guilford Press.

Horvath, A. O., & Symonds, B. D. (1991). Relation between working alliance and outcome in psychotherapy: A meta-analysis. *Journal of Counseling Psychology, 38*(2), 139–149.

Hoshmand, L. T., & Martin, J. (1995). The inquiry process. In L. T. Hoshmand & J. Martin (Eds.), *Research as praxis: Lessons from programmatic research in therapeutic psychology. Counseling and development series.* (pp. 29–47). New York: Teachers College Press.

Hout, M. A., Emmelkamp, P. M. G., Kraaykamp, J., & Griez, E. (1988). Behavioural treatment of obsessive-compulsives: Inpatient versus outpatient. *Behaviour Research and Therapy, 26,* 331–332.

Howard, G. S. (1985). Can research in the human sciences become more relevant to practice? *Journal of Counseling and Development, 63,* 539–544.

Howard, K. I., Davidson, C. V., O'Mahoney, M. T., Orlinsky, D. E., & Brown, K. P. (1989). Patterns of psychotherapy utilization. *American Journal of Psychiatry, 146,* 775–778.

Howard, K. I., Kopta, S. M., Krause, M. S., & Orlinsky, D. E. (1986). The dose-effect relationship in psychotherapy [Special issue: Psychotherapy research]. *American Psychologist, 41*(2), 159–164.

Howard, K. I., Moras, K., Brill, P. L., Martinovich, Z., & Lutz, W. (1996). Evaluation of psychotherapy: Efficacy, effectiveness, and patient progress. *American Psychologist, 51,* 1059–1064.

Hoyt, K. B., & Lester, J. A. (1994). *Learning to work: NCDA Gallup Survey.* Alexandra VA: National Career Development Association

Hughey, K. F., Gysbers, N. C., & Starr, M. (1993). Evaluating comprehensive school guidance programs: Assessing the perceptions of students, parents, and teachers. *School Counselor, 41*(1), 31–35.

Hughey, K. F., Lapan, R. T., & Gysbers, N. C. (1993). Evaluating a high school guidance-language arts career unit: A qualitative approach. *The School Counselor, 41,* 96–101.

Hunt, D. D., Carr, J. E., Dagadakis, C. S., & Walker, E. A. (1985). Cognitive match as a predictor of psychotherapy outcome. *Psychotherapy, 22,* 718–721.

Hutchinson, N. L., Freeman, J. G., Downey, K. H., & Kilbreath, L. (1992). Development and evaluation of an instructional module to promote career maturity for youth with learning difficulties. *Canadian Journal of Counselling, 26*(4), 290–299.

Iberg, J. R. (1991). Applying statistical control theory to bring together clinical supervision and psychotherapy research. *Journal of Consulting and Clinical Psychology, 59,* 575–586.

Imbimbo, P. V. (1994). Integrating personal and career counseling: A challenge for counselors. *Journal of Employment Counseling, 31,* 50–59.

Institute of Medicine. (1989). *Research on children and adolescents with mental, behavioral, and developmental disorders.* Washington, DC: National Academy Press.

Jackson, L., & Elliott, R. (1990, June). *Is experiential therapy effective in treating depression? Initial outcome data.* Paper presented at the annual meeting of Society for Psychotherapy Research, Wintergreen, VA.

Jacobson, N. S., Dobson, K., Fluzetti, A. E., Schmaling, K. B., & Salusky, S. (1991). Marital therapy as a treatment for depression. *Journal of Consulting and Clinical Psychology, 59,* 547–557.

Jacobson, N. S., Follette, W. C., & Revenstorf, D. (1984). Psychotherapy outcome research: Methods for reporting variability and evaluation clinical significance. *Behavior Therapy, 15,* 336–352.

Johnson, M. (1988, June). *Construct validation of the therapeutic alliance.* Paper presented at the annual meeting of the Society for Psychotherapy Research, Santa Fe, NM.

Jones, E. E. (1982). Psychotherapists' impressions of treatment outcome as a function of race. *Journal of Clinical Psychology, 38*(4), 722–732.

Jones, E. E., Cummings, J. D., & Horowitz, M. J. (1988). Another look at the nonspecific hypothesis of therapeutic effectiveness. *Journal of Consulting and Clinical Psychology, 56*(1), 48–55.

Jones, E. E., Krupnick, J. H., & Kerig, P. K. (1987). Some gender effects in brief psychotherapy. *Psychotherapy, 24,* 207–212.

Jones, E. E., Parke, L. A., & Pulos, S. M. (1992). How therapy is conducted in the private consultation room: A multidimensional description of brief psychodynamic treatments. *Psychotherapy Research, 2,* 16–30.

Jones, E. E., Wynne, M. F., & Watson, D. D. (1986). Client perception of treatment in crisis intervention and longer-term psychotherapies. *Psychotherapy, 23,* 120–132.

Jones, E. E., & Zoppel, C. L. (1982). Impact of client and therapist gender on psychotherapy process and outcome. *Journal of Consulting and Clinical Psychology, 50*(2), 259–272.

Jorm, A. F. (1989). Modifiability of trait anxiety and neuroticism: A meta-analysis of the literature. *Australian and New Zealand Journal of Psychiatry, 23,* 21–29.

Kadera, S. W., Lambert, M. J., & Andrews, A. A. (1996). How much therapy is really enough: A session-by-session analysis of the psychotherapy dose-effect relationship. *Journal of Psychotherapy: Practice and Research, 5,* 1-22.

Kanfer, F. H. (1990). The scientist-practitioner connection: A bridge in need of constant attention. *Professional Psychology: Research and Practice, 21,* 264–270.

Kasvikis, Y., & Marks, I. M. (1988). Clomipramine, self-exposure, and therapist-accompanied exposure in obsessive-compulsive ritualizers: Two-year follow-up. *Journal of Anxiety Disorders, 2*(4), 291–298.

Kazdin, A. E. (1980). Acceptability of alternative treatment for deviant child behavior. *Journal of Applied Behavior Analysis, 13,* 259–273.

Kazdin, A. E. (1981). Drawing valid inferences from case studies. *Journal of Consulting and Clinical Psychology, 49,* 183–192.

Kazdin, A. E. (1983). Failure of persons to respond to the token economy. In E. B. Foa & P. M. G. Emmelkamp (Eds.), *Failures in behavior therapy* (pp. 335-354). New York: Wiley.

Kazdin, A. E. (1986). Research designs and methodology. In S. L. Garfield & A. E. Bergin (Eds.), *Handbook of psychotherapy and behavioral change* (pp. 23–68). New York: Wiley.

Kazdin, A. E. (1987). Treatment of antisocial behavior in children: Current status and future directions. *Psychological Bulletin, 102,* 187–203.

Kazdin, A. E. (1991). Effectiveness of psychotherapy with children and adolescents [Special section: Clinical child psychology: Perspectives on child and adolescent therapy]. *Journal of Consulting and Clinical Psychology, 59*(6), 785–798.

Kazdin, A. E. (1993). Psychotherapy for children and adolescents: Current progress and future research direction. *American Psychologist, 48,* 644–657.

Kazdin, A. E. (1994). Methodology, design, and evaluation in psychotherapy research. In A. E. Bergin & S. L. Garfield (Eds.), *Handbook of psychotherapy and behavior change* (pp. 19–71). New York: Wiley.

Kazdin, A. E., Bass, D., Siegel, T. C., & Thomas, C. (1989). Cognitive-behavioral therapy and relationship therapy in the treatment of children referred for antisocial behavior. *Journal of Consulting and Clinical Psychology, 57,* 522–535.

Kazdin, A. E., Esveldt-Dawson, K., French, N. H., & Unis, A. S. (1987). Problem-solving skills training and relationship therapy in the treatment of antisocial child behavior. *Journal of Consulting and Clinical Psychology, 55,* 76–85.

Kazdin, A. E., Siegel, T. C., & Bass, D. (1992). Cognitive problem-solving skills training and parent mangement training in the treatment of antisocial behavior in children. *Journal of Consulting and Clinical Psychology, 60,* 733–747.

Kelly, T. A. (1990). The role of values in psychotherapy: Review and methodological critique. *Clinical Psychology Review, 10,* 171–186.

Kendall, P. C., Ronan, K. R., & Epps, J. (1991). Agression in children/adolescents: Cognitive-behavioral treatment perspectives. In D. J. Pepler & K. H. Rubin (Eds.), *The development and treatment of childhood aggression* (pp. 341–360). Hillsdale, NJ: Erlbaum.

Kerr, B. A., & Erb, C. (1991). Career counseling with academically talented students: Effects of a value-based intervention. *Journal of Counseling Psychology, 38*(3), 309–314.

Kerr, B. A., & Ghrist-Priebe, S. L. (1988). Intervention for multipotentiality: Effects of a career counseling laboratory for gifted high school students. *Journal of Counseling and Development, 66,* 366–369.

Kiesler, D. J., & Watkins, L. M. (1989). Interpersonal complementarity and the therapeutic alliance: A study of relationship in psychotherapy. *Psychotherapy, 26*(2), 183–194.

Kiresuk, T. J., & Sherman, R. E. (1968). Goal attainment scaling: A general method for evaluating comprehensive community health programs. *Community Mental Health Journal, 4,* 443–453.

Kirschner, T., Hoffman, M. A., & Hill, C. E. (1994). Case study of the process and outcome of career counseling. *Journal of Counseling Psychology, 41,* 216–236.

Klee, M. R., Abeles, N., & Muller, R. T. (1990). Therapeutic alliance: Early indicators, course, and outcome. *Psychotherapy, 27*(2), 166–174.

Kokotovic, A. M., & Tracey, T. J. (1987). Premature termination at a university counseling center. *Journal of Counseling Psychology, 34,* 80–87.

Kopta, S. M., Howard, K. I., Lowry, J. L., & Beutler, L. E. (1994). Patterns of symptomatic recovery in psychotherapy. *Journal of Consulting and Clinical Psychology, 62,* 1009–1016.

Koran, L., & Costell, R. (1973). Early termination from group psychotherapy. *International Journal of Group Psychotherapy, 23,* 346–359.

Krumboltz, J. D., Becker-Haven, J. F., & Burnett, K. F. (1979). Counseling psychology. *Annual Review of Psychology, 30,* 555–602.

Krumboltz, J. E. (1993). Integrating career and personal counseling. *Career Development Quarterly, 42,* 143–148.

Kulka, R. A., Veroff, J., & Douvan, E. (1979). Social class and the use of professional help for personal problems: 1957–1976. *Journal of Health and Social Behavior, 20,* 2–17.

Kush, K., & Cochran, L. (1993). Enhancing a sense of agency through career planning. *Journal of Counseling Psychology, 40,* 434-439.

LaCrosse, M. B. (1980). Perceived counselor social influence and counseling outcomes: Validity of the Counselor Rating Form. *Journal of Counseling Psychology, 27*(4), 320-327.

Lafferty, P., Beutler, L. E., & Crago, M. (1989). Differences between more and less effective psychotherapists: A study of select therapist variables. *Journal of Consulting and Clinical Psychology, 57*(1), 76–80.

Lambert, M. J. (1976). Spontaneous remission in adult neurotic disorders: A revision and summary. *Psychological Bulletin, 83*(1), 107–119.

Lambert, M. J. (1983). Introduction to assessment of psychotherapy outcome: Historical perspective and current issues. In M. J. Lambert, E. R. Christensen, & S. S. DeJulio (Eds.), *The assessment of psychotherapy outcome* (pp. 3–32). New York: Wiley-Interscience.

Lambert, M. J. (1986). Some implications of psychotherapy research for eclectic practice. *International Journal of Eclectic Psychotherapy, 5,* 16–46.

Lambert, M. J. (1989). The individual therapist's contribution to psychotherapy process and outcome [Special issue: Psychotherapy process research]. *Clinical Psychology Review, 9*(4), 469–485.

Lambert, M. J. (1991). Introduction to psychotherapy research. In L. E. Beutler & M.Crago (Eds.), *Psychotherapy research: An international review of programmatic studies* (pp. 1–23). Washington, DC: American Psychological Association.

Lambert, M. J., & Bergin, A. E. (1983). Therapist characteristics and their contribution to psychotherapy outcome. In C. E. Walker (Ed.), *The handbook of clinical psychology: Theory, research and practice* (pp. 205-241). Homewood, IL: Dow Jones-Irwin.

Lambert, M. J., & Bergin, A. E. (1994). The effectiveness of psychotherapy. In A. E. Bergin & S. L. Garfield (Eds.), *Handbook of psychotherapy and behavior change* (pp. 143–189). New York: Wiley.

Lambert, M. J., & Cattani-Thompson, K. (1996). Current findings regarding the effectiveness of counseling: Implications for practice. *Journal of Counseling and Development, 74,* 601–608.

Lambert, M. J., Hatch, D. R., Kingston, M. D., & Edwards, B. C. (1986). Zung, Beck, and Hamilton Rating Scales as measures of treatment outcome: A meta-analytic comparison [Special issue: Psychotherapy research]. *Journal of Consulting and Clinical Psychology, 54*(1), 54–59.

Lambert, M. J., & Hill, C. E. (1994). Methodological issues in studying psychotherapy process and outcome. In A. E. Bergin & S. L. Garfield (Eds.), *Handbook of psychotherapy and behavior change* (pp. 72–113). New York: Wiley.

Lambert, M. J., Masters, K. S., & Ogles, B. M. (1991). Outcome research in counseling. In C. E. Watkins & L. J. Schneider (Eds.), *Research in counseling* (pp. 51–83). Hillsdale, NJ: Erlbaum.

Lambert, M. J., & Ogles, B. M. (1988). Treatment manuals: Problems and promise. *Journal of Integrative and Eclectic Psychotherapy, 7*(2), 187–204.

Lambert, M. J., Ogles, B. M., & Masters, K. S. (1992). Choosing outcome assessment devices: An organizational and conceptual scheme. *Journal of Counseling & Development, 70,* 527–532.

Lambert, M. J., Shapiro, D. A., & Bergin, A. E. (1986). The effectiveness of psychotherapy. In S. L.Garfield & A. E. Bergin (Eds.), *Handbook of psychotherapy and behavior change* (p. 157–211). New York: Wiley.

Lambert, M. J., Weber, F. D., & Stykes, J. D. (1993, April). *Psychotherapy versus placebo.* Poster presented at the annual meeting of the Western Psychological Association, Phoenix, AZ.

Lapan, R. T., Gysbers, N., Hughey, K., & Arni, T. J. (1993). Evaluating a guidance and language arts unit for high school juniors. *Journal of Counseling and Development, 71,* 444–451.

Lavoritano, J. E., & Segal, P. B. (1992). Evaluating the efficacy of short-term counseling on adolescents in a school setting. *Adolescence, 27*(107), 535–543.

Leary, T. (1957). *Interpersonal diagnosis of personality.* New York: Roland.

Lee, R. S. (1993). Effects of classroom guidance on student achievement. *Elementary School Guidance and Counseling, 27,* 163–171.

Lenz, J. G., Reardon, R. C., & Sampson, J. P. (1993). Holland's theory and effective use of computer-assisted career guidance systems. *Journal of Career Development, 19*(4), 245–253.

Leso, J. F., & Neimeyer, G. J. (1991). Role of gender and construct type in vocational complexity and choice of academic major. *Journal of Counseling Psychology, 38*(2), 182–188.

Libby, R. (1976). Man versus model of man: Some conflicting evidence. *Organizational Behavior and Human Performance, 16*(1), 1–12.

Liberman, B. L. (1978). The role of mastery in psychotherapy: Maintenance of improvement and prescriptive change. In J. D. Frank, R. Hoehn-Saric, S. D. Imber, B. L. Liberman, & A. R. Stone (Eds.), *Effective ingredients of successful psychotherapy.* New York: Brunner/Mazel.

Lindsay, W. R., Gramsu, C. V., McLaughlin, E., Hood, E., & Espie, C. A. (1987). A controlled trial of treatment for generalized anxiety disorder. *British Journal of Clinical Psychology, 26,* 3–15.

Littrell, J. M., Malia, J. A., & Vanderwood, M. (1995). Single-session brief counseling in a high school. *Journal of Counseling and Development, 73,* 451–458.

Loesch, L., & Vacc, N. (Eds.) (1977). *Research in counseling and therapy.* Greensboro, NC: ERIC Counseling and Student Services Clearinghouse, University of North Carolina at Greensboro.

Loftus, E. F. (1993). The reality of repressed memories. *American Psychologist, 48,* 518–537.

Luborsky, L., Chandler, N., Auerbach, A. H., Cohen, J., & Bachrach, H. M. (1971). Factors influencing the outcome of psychotherapy: A review of quantitative research. *Psychological Bulletin, 75,* 145–185.

Luborsky, L., Crits-Christoph, P., McLellan, A. T., Woody, G., Piper, W., Liberman, B., Imber, S., & Pilkonis, P. (1986). Do therapists vary much in their success: Findings from four outcome studies. *American Journal of Orthopsychiatry, 56*(4), 501–512.

Luborsky, L., Crits-Christoph, P., Mintz, J., & Auerbach, A. (1988). Who will benefit from psychotherapy? *Predicting therapeutic outcomes.* New York: Basic Books.

Luborsky, L., McLellan, A. T., Woody, G. E., O'Brien, C. P., & Auerbach, A. (1985). Therapist success and its determinants. *Archives of General Psychiatry, 42*(6), 602–611.

Luborsky, L., Mintz, J., Auerbach, A., Crits-Christoph, P., Bachrach, H., Todd, T., Johnson, M., Cohen, M., & O'Brien, C. P. (1980). Predicting the outcome of psychotherapy: Findings of the Penn Psychotherapy Project. *Archives of General Psychiatry, 37*, 471–481.

Luborsky, L., Singer, B., & Luborsky, L. (1975). Comparative studies of psychotherapies: Is it true that "everyone has won and all must have prizes"? *Archives of General Psychiatry, 32*(8), 995–1008.

Lyons, L. C., & Woods, P. J. (1991). The efficacy of rational-emotive therapy: A quantitative review of the outcome research. *Clinical Psychology Review, 11*(4), 357–369.

Mahoney, J. S., & Merritt, S. R. (1993). Educational hopes of black and white high school seniors in Virginia. *Journal of Educational Research, 87*(1), 31–38.

Mahrer, A. R. (1988). Discovery-oriented psychotherapy research: Rationale, aims, and methods. *American Psychologist, 43*(9), 694–702.

Mallinckrodt, B., & Helms, J. E. (1986). Effect of disabled counselors' self-disclosures on client perceptions of the counselor. *Journal of Counseling Psychology, 33*, 343–348.

Mann, A. H., Jenkins, R., & Belsey, E. (1981). The twelve-month outcome of patients with neurotic illness in general practice. *Psychological Medicine, 11*(3), 535–550.

Marin, P. A., & Splete, H. (1991). A comparison of the effect of two computer-based counseling interventions on the career decidedness of adults. *Career Development Quarterly, 39*(4), 360–371.

Marshall, C., & Rossman, G. B. (1989). *Designing qualitative research.* Newbury Park, CA: Sage.

Marshall, W. L., Bristol, D., & Barbaree, H. E. (1992). Cognitions and courage in the avoidance behavior of acrophobics. *Behaviour Research and Therapy, 30*, 463–470.

Marshall, W. L., & Segal, Z. V. (1990). Drugs combined with behavioral psychotherapy. In A. S. Bellack, M. Hersen, & A. E. Kazdin (Eds.), *International handbook of behavior modification and therapy* (pp. 267–279). New York: Plenum.

Marten, P. A., & Heimberg, R. G. (1995). Toward an integration of independent practice and clinical research. *Professional Psychology: Research and Practice, 26*,48–53.

Martin, J., & Hoshmand, L. T. (1995). Research on psychological practice. In L. T. Hoshmand & J. Martin (Eds.), *Research as praxis: Lessons from programmatic research in therapeutic psychology,* (pp. 48–80). New York: Teachers College Press.

Martin, P. J., & Sterne, A. L. (1976). Post-hospital adjustment as related to therapists' in-therapy behavior. *Psychotherapy Theory, Research and Practice, 13*(3), 267–273.

Mathews, A. M., Johnston, D. W., Shaw, P. M., & Gelder, M. G. (1974). Process variables and the prediction of outcome in behaviour therapy. *The British Journal of Psychiatry, 125,* 256–264.

Mattick, R. P., Peters, L., & Clarke, J. C. (1989). Exposure and cognitive restructuring for social phobia: A controlled study. *Behavior Therapy, 20*(1), 3–23.

Mau, W. C., & Jepsen, D. A. (1992). Effects of computer-assisted instruction in using formal decision-making strategies to choose a college major. *Journal of Counseling Psychology, 39*(2), 185–192.

McAuliffe, G., & Fredrickson, R. (1990). The effects of program length and participant characteristics on group. *Journal of Employment Counseling, 27*(1), 19–22.

McCullough, L., Winston, A., Farber, B. A., Porter, F., Pollack, J., Laikin, M., Vingiano, W., & Truillo, M. (1991). The relationship of patient-therapist interaction to outcome in brief psychotherapy. *Psychotherapy, 28*(4), 525–533.

McLean, P. D., & Hakstain, A. R. (1990). Relative endurance of unipolar depression treatment effects: Longitudinal follow-up. *Journal of Consulting and Clinical Psychology, 58*(4), 482–488.

McLean, P. D., & Taylor, S. (1992). Severity of unipolar depression and choice of treatment. *Behavior Research and Therapy, 30,* 443–451.

McLellan, A. T., Woody, G. E., Luborsky, L., & Goehl, L. (1988). Is the counselor an "active ingredient" in substance abuse rehabilitation? *The Journal of Nervous and Mental Disease, 179,* (No. 7) 423–430.

McMahon, R. J., & Wells, K. C. (1989). Conduct disorders. In E. J. Mash & R. A. Barkley (Eds.), *Treatment of childhood disorders* (pp. 73–132). New York: Guilford Press.

McNeill, B. W., May, R. J., & Lee, V. E. (1987). Perceptions of counselor source characteristics by premature and successful teminators. *Journal of Counseling Psychology, 34*(1), 86–89.

Mersch, P. P., Emmelkamp, P. M. G., & Lips, C. (1991). Social phobia: Individual response patterns and the long-term effects of behavioral and cognitive interventions. A follow-up study. *Behaviour Research and Therapy, 29*(4), 357–362.

Meyer, A. E. (1981). The Hamburg Short Psychotherapy Comparison Experiment. *Psychotherapy and Psychosomatics, 35,* 77–270.

Miller, I. W., Norman, W. H., Keitner, G. I., Bishop, S. B., & Dow, M. G. (1989). Cognitive-behavioral treatment of depressed inpatients. *Behavior Therapy, 20,* 25–47.

Miller, M. J. (1992). Synthesizing results from an interest and personality inventory to improve career decision making. *Journal of Employment Counseling, 29*(2), 50–59.

Miller, R. C., & Berman, J. S. (1983). The efficacy of cognitive behavior therapies: A quantitative review of the research evidence. *Psychological Bulletin, 94*(1), 39–53.

Mischel, W. (1977). On the future of personality research. *American Psychologist, 32,* 246–254.

Mitchell, K. M., Bozarth, J. D., & Kraft, C. C. (1977). A reappraisal of the therapeutic effectiveness of accurate empathy, non-possessive warmth, and genuineness. In A. S. Gurman & A. M. Razin (Eds.), *Effective psychotherapy* (pp. 482-502). New York: Pergamon Press.

Mohl, P. C., Martinez, D., Ticknor, C., Huang, M., & Cordell, M. D. (1991). Early dropouts from psychotherapy. *Journal of Nervous and Mental Disease, 179*(8), 478–481.

Moncher, F. J., & Prinz, R. J. (1991). Treatment fidelity in outcome studies. *Clinical Psychology Review, 11,* 247–266.

Monette, D. R., Sullivan, T. J., & DeJong, C. R. (1990). *Applied social research: Tool for the human services.* Fort Worth, TX: Holt, Rinehart & Winston.

Morey, R. E., Miller, C. D., Rosen, L. A., & Fulton, R. (1993). High school peer counseling: The relationship between student satisfaction and peer counselors' style of helping. *The School Counselor, 40,* 293–300.

Morgan, R., Luborsky, L., Crits-Christoph, P., Curtis, H., & Soloman, J. (1982). Predicting the outcomes of psychotherapy by the Penn Helping Alliance Rating Method. *Archives of General Psychiatry, 39*(4), 397–402.

Morrison, J. A., Olivos, K., Domingues, G., Gomez, D., & Lena, D. (1993). The application of family systems approaches to school behavior problems on a school-level discipline board: An outcome study. *Elementary School Guidance & Counseling, 27,* 258–272.

Morrow-Bradley, C., & Elliott, R. (1986). Utilization of psychotherapy research by practicing psychotherapists. *American Psychologist, 41,* 188–197.

Moses-Zirkes, S. (1993, May). Outcome research: Everybody wants it. *APA Monitor,* pp. 22–23.

Myers, R. A. (1986). Research on educational and vocational counseling. In S. L. Garfield & A. E. Bergin (Eds.), *Handbook of psychotherapy and behavior change* (pp. 715–738). New York: Wiley.

Nearpass, E. L. (1990). Counseling and guidance effectiveness in North American high schools: A meta-analysis of the research findings (Doctoral dissertation, University of Colorado at Boulder, 1989). *Dissertation Abstracts International, 50,* 1984A.

Neimeyer, R. A., Robinson, L. A., Berman, J. S., & Haykal, R. F. (1989). Clinical outcome of group therapies for depression. *Group Analysis, 22,* 73–86.

Nelson, M. L., & Allstetter-Neufeldt, S. (1996). Building on an empirical foundation: Strategies to enhance good practice. *Journal of Counseling & Development, 74,* 609–615.

Nevo, O. (1990). Career counseling from the counselee perspective: Analysis of feedback. *Career Development Quarterly, 38*(4), 314–324.

Nicholson, R. A., & Berman, J. S. (1983). Is follow-up necessary in evaluating psychotherapy? *Psychological Bulletin, 93*(2), 261–278.

Nietzel, M. T., Russel, R. L., Hemmings, K. A., & Gretten, M. L. (1987). Clinical significance of psychotherapy for unipolar depression: A meta-analytic approach to social comparison. *Journal of Consulting and Clinical Psychology, 55*(2), 156–161.

Niles, S. G. (1993). The timing of counselor contact in the use of a computer information delivery. *Journal of Employment Counseling, 30*(1), 2–12.

Niles, S. G., & Garis, J. W. (1990). The effects of a career planning course and a computer-assisted career guidance program (SIGI PLUS) on undecided university students. *Journal of Career Development, 16,* 237–248.

Norcross, J. C., & Grencavage, L. M. (1989). Integration and eclecticism in psychotherapy: Major themes and obstacles. *British Journal of Guidance and Counselling, 17,* 227–247.

Norcross, J. C., Prochaska, J. O., & Gallagher, K. M. (1989). Clinical psychologists in the 1980s: II. Theory, research and practice. *The Clinical Psychologist, 42*(3), 45–53.

Ogles, B. M., Lambert, M. J., Weight, D. G., & Payne, I. R. (1990). Agoraphobia outcome measurement: A review and meta-analysis. *Psychological Assessment, 2*(3), 317–325.

Ogles, B. M., Sawyer, J. D., & Lambert, M. J. (1993, June). *The clinical significance of the NIMH Treatment of Depression Collaborative Research Program data.* Paper presented at the annual meeting of the Society of Psychotherapy Research, Pittsburgh, PA.

O'Leary, K. D., & Beach, S. R. H. (1990). Marital therapy: A viable treatment for depression and marital discord. *American Journal of Psychiatry, 47,* 183–186.

Oliver, L. W., & Spokane, A. R. (1988). Career-intervention outcome: What contributes to client gain? *Journal of Counseling Psychology, 35*(4), 447–462.

Oliver, L. W., Whiston, S. C., Sexton, T. L., Lasoff, D. L., & Spokane, A. R. (1996, August). *Career intervention: Major themes and future research.* Paper presented at the annual meeting of the American Psychological Association, Toronto, Canada.

Omizo, M. M., & Omizo, S. A. (1988). The effects of participation in group counseling sessions on self-esteem and locus of control among adolescents from divorced families. *School Counselor, 36*(1), 54–60.

Orlinsky, D. E., Grawe, D., & Parks, B. K. (1994). Process and outcome in psychotherapy—NOCH EINMAL. In A. E. Bergin & S. L. Garfield (Eds.), *Handbook of psychotherapy and behavior change* (pp. 270–378). New York: Wiley.

Orlinsky, D. E., & Howard, K. I. (1980). Gender and psychotherapeutic outcome. In A. M. Brodsky & R. Hare-Mustin (Eds.), *Women and psychotherapy: An assessment of research and practice* (pp. 3–34). New York: Guilford Press.

Orlinsky, D. E., & Howard, K. I. (1986). Process and outcome in psychotherapy. In S. L. Garfield & A. E. Bergin (Eds.), *Handbook of psychotherapy and behavior change* (3rd ed., pp. 361–381). New York: Wiley.

Osipow, S. H., Carney, C. G., Winer, J., Yanico, B., & Koschier, M. (1976). *Career Decision Scale - Third Revision.* Odessa, FL: Psychological Assessment Resources.

Ost, L. G. (1988). Applied relaxation in the treatment of panic disorder [Special issue: Applied relaxation: Method and applications]. *Scandinavian Journal of Behaviour Therapy, 17*(2), 111–124.

Ost, L. G., Fellenius, J., & Sterner, K. (1991). Applied tension, exposure in vivo, and tension-only in the treatment of blood phobia. *Behavior Research and Therapy, 29,* 561–574.

Ost, L. G., Sterner, U., & Fellenius, J. (1989). Applied tension, applied relaxation in the treatment of blood phobia. *Behaviour Research and Therapy, 27,* 109.

Paivio, S., & Greenberg, L. S. (1992, May). *Resolving unfinished business: A study of effects.* Paper presented at the annual meeting of the Society for Psychotherapy Research, Berkeley, CA.

Palmer, S., & Cochran, L. (1988). Parents as agents of career development. *Journal of Counseling Psychology, 35*(1), 71–76.

Parsons, F. (1909). *Choosing a vocation.* Boston: Houghton Mifflin.

Patton, M. J. (1989). Problems with the alternatives to the use of coding schemes in research and counseling. *Counseling Psychologist, 17,* 490–506.

Patton, M. Q. (1990). *Qualitative evaluation and research methods.* Newbury Park, CA: Sage.

Peca-Baker, T. A., & Friedlander, M. L. (1989). Why are self-disclosing counselors attractive? *Journal of Counseling and Development, 67,* 279–282.

Perotti, L. P., & Hopewell, C. A. (1980). Expectancy effects in psychotherapy and systematic desensitization: A review. *JSAS: Catalog of Selected Documents in Psychology, 10*(Ms. No. 2052).

Perry, N. S. (1993). School counseling. In G. R. Walz & J. C. Bleuer (Eds.), *Counselor efficacy: Assessing and using counseling outcome research* (pp. 37–49). Ann Arbor, MI: Educational Resources and Information Center.

Person, J. (1989). *Cognitive therapy in practice.* New York: W. W. Norton.

Persons, J. B. (1991). Psychotherapy outcome studies do not accurately represent current models of psychotherapy: A proposed remedy. *American Psychologist, 46*(2), 99–106.

Persons, J. B., Burns, D. D., & Perloff, J. M. (1988). Predictors of dropout and outcome in cognitive therapy for depression in a private practice setting. *Cognitive Therapy and Research, 12*(6), 557–575.

Persons, R. W., & Pepinsky, H. B. (1966). Convergence in psychotherapy with delinquent boys. *Journal of Counseling Psychology, 13,* 329–334.

Peterson, D. R. (1995). The reflective educator. *American Psychologist, 50,* 975–983.

Phillips, E. L., & Fagen, P. J. (1982, August). *Attrition: Focus on the intake and first therapy interviews.* Paper presented at the 90th annual convention of the American Psychological Association, Washington, DC.

Phillips, S. D., Friedlander, M. L., Kost, P. P., Specterman, R. V., & Robbins, E. S. (1988). Personal versus vocational focus in career counseling: A retrospective outcome. *Journal of Counseling and Development, 67*(3), 169–173.

Pickering, J. W., & Vacc, N. A. (1984). Effectiveness of career development interventions for college students: A review of published research. *Vocational Guidance Quarterly, 32*(3), 149–159.

Pilkonis, P. A., Imber, S. D., Lewis, P., & Rubinsky, P. (1984). A comparative outcome study of individual, group, and conjoint psychotherapy. *Archives of General Psychiatry, 41,* 431–437.

Piper, W. E., Azim, H. F., Joyce, A. S., & McCallum, M. (1991). Transference interpretations, therapeutic alliance, and outcome in short-term individual psychotherapy. *Archives of General Psychiatry, 48*(10), 946–953.

Power, K. G., Simpson, R. J., Swanson, V., & Wallace, L. A. (1990). A controlled comparison of cognitive-behavior therapy, diazepam, and placebo, alone and in combination, for the treatment of generalized anxiety disorder. *Journal of Anxiety Disorders, 4,* 267–292.

Prioleau, L., Murdock, M., & Brody, N. (1983). An analysis of psychotherapy versus placebo studies. *Behavioral and Brain Sciences, 6*(2), 275–310.

Prochaska, J. O. (1991). Prescribing to the stage and level of phobic patients. *Psychotherapy, 28*(3), 463–468.

Prochaska, J. O., Velicer, W. F., DiClemente, C. C., & Fava, J. (1988). Measuring processes of change: Application to the cessation of smoking. *Journal of Consulting and Clinical Psychology, 56*(4), 520–528.

Propst, L. R. (1980). The comparative efficacy of religious and nonreligious imagery for the treatment of mild depression in religious individuals. *Cognitive Therapy and Research, 4,* 167–178.

Propst, L. R., Ostrom, R., Watkins, P., Dean, T., & Mashburn, D. (1992). Comparative efficacy of religious and nonreligious cognitive-behavioral therapy for the treatment of clinical depression in religious individuals. *Journal of Consulting Clinical Psychology, 60,* 94–103.

Prout, H. T., & DeMartino, R. A. (1986). A meta-analysis of school-based studies of psychotherapy. *Journal of School Psychology, 24,* 285–292.

Quintana, S. M., & Holahan, W. (1992). Termination in short-term counseling: Comparison of successful and unsuccessful cases. *Journal of Counseling Psychology, 39,* 299–305.

Quintana, S. M., & Meara, N. M. (1990). Internalization of therapeutic relationships in short-term psychotherapy. *Journal of Counseling Psychology, 37*(2), 123–130.

Rabin, A. S., Kaslow, N. J., & Rehm, L. P. (1985). Factors influencing continuation in a behavioral therapy. *Behaviour Research and Therapy, 23,* 695–698.

Rachman, S., & Levitt, K. (1988). Panic, fear reduction and habituation. *Behaviour Research and Therapy, 26,* 199–206.

Rathvon, N. W. (1991). Effects of a guidance unit in two formats on the examination performance of underachieving middle school students. *School Counselor, 38*(4), 294–304.

Reams, R., & Friedrich, W. (1994). The efficacy of time-limited play therapy with maltreated preschoolers. *Journal of Clinical Psychology, 50,* 889–899.

Rice, D. P., Kelman, S., Miller, L. S., & Dunmeyer, S. (1990). *The economic costs of alcohol and drug abuse and mental illness: 1985* (Report from the Office of Financing and Coverage Policy of the Alcohol, Drug Abuse, and Mental Health Administration, U. S. Department of Health and Human Services). San Francisco, CA: Institute for Health and Aging, University of California.

Robinson, L. A., Berman, J. S., & Neimeyer, R. A. (1990). Psychotherapy for the treatment of depression: A comprehensive review of controlled outcome research. *Psychological Bulletin, 108,* 30–49.

Rodriguez, M., & Blocher, D. (1988). A comparison of two approaches to enhancing career maturity in Puerto Rican college women. *Journal of Counseling Psychology, 35,* 275–280.

Rogers, C. (1957). The necessary and sufficient conditions of therapeutic personality change. *Journal of Consulting Psychology, 21,* 95–103.

Rose, C. C., & Rose, S. D. (1992). Family change groups for the early school age child. *Special Services in the Schools, 6*(3-4), 113–127.

Rosenthal, D., & Frank, J. D. (1956). Psychotherapy and the placebo effect. *Psychological Bulletin, 53,* 294–302.

Rosenthal, R. (1994). *Meta-analytic procedures for social research.* Newbury Park, CA: Sage.

Rounsaville, B. J., Weissear, M. M., & Prusoff, B. A. (1981). Psychotherapy with depressed outpatients. Patient and process variables as predictors of outcome. *British Journal of Psychiatry, 138,* 67–74.

Ruiter, C., de Rijken, H., Garssen, B., & Kraaimaat, F. (1989). Breathing retraining, exposure and a combination of both in the treatment of panic disorder with agoraphobia. *Behaviour Research and Therapy, 27,* 647–655.

Sachs, J. S. (1983). Negative factors in brief psychotherapy: An empirical assessment. *Journal of Consulting and Clinical Psychology, 51*(4), 557–564.

Safran, J. D., & Wallner, L. K. (1991). The relative predictive validity of two therapeutic alliance measures in cognitive therapy. *Psychological Assessment, 3*(2), 188–195.

Saunders, S. M., Howard, K. I., & Orlinsky, D. E. (1989). The Therapeutic Bond Scales: Psychometric characteristics and relationship to treatment effectiveness. *Psychological Assessment, 1*(4), 323–330.

Schindler, L. (1991). *Die empirische Analyse der therapeutischen Beziehung. Beitrage zur Prozessforschung in der Verhaltenstherapie* [The empirical analysis of the therapeutic relation: Contributions to process research in behavior therapy]. Berlin, Heidelberg: Springer-Verlag.

Schmidt, J. J. (1995). Assessing school counseling programs through external reviews. *The School Counselor, 43,* 114–115.

Scholing, A., & Emmelkamp, P. M. G. (1989). Individualized treatment for social phobia. In P. M. G. Emmelkamp, W. Everaerd, F. Kraaimaat, & M. Van Son (Eds.), *Fresh perspectives on anxiety disorders* (pp. 213–228). Amsterdam: Swets.

Scholing, A., & Emmelkamp, P. M. G. (1993a). Cognitive and behavioral treatments of fear of blushing, sweating or trembling. *Behaviour Research and Therapy, 31,* 155–170.

Scholing, A., & Emmelkamp, P. M. G. (1993b). Exposure with and without cognitive therapy for generalized social phobia: Effects of individual and group treatment. *Behaviour Research & Therapy, 31*(7), 667–681.

Schulte, D., & Kunzel, R. (1991, May). *Relevance and meaning of the therapist's control.* Paper presented at the 22nd Annual Meeting of the Society for Psychotherapy Research, Lyon, France.

Seligman, M. E. P. (1995). The effectiveness of psychotherapy: The Consumer Reports study. *American Psychologist, 50,* 965–974.

Seligman, M. E. P. (1996). Science as an ally of practice. *American Psychologist, 51,* 1072–1079.

Sexton, T. L. (1996). The relevance of counseling outcome research: Current trends and practical implications. *Journal of Counseling and Development, 74,* 590–600.

Sexton, T. L., Montgomery, D., Goff, K., & Nugent, W. (1993). Ethical, therapeutic, and legal considerations in the use of paradoxical techniques: The emerging debate. *Journal of Mental Health Counseling, 15*(3), 260–277.

Sexton, T. L., & Whiston, S. C. (1991). A review of the empirical basis for counseling: Implications for practice and training. *Counselor Education and Supervision, 30,* 330–354.

Sexton, T. L., & Whiston, S. C. (1994). The status of the counseling relationship: An empirical review, theoretical implications, and research directions. *The Counseling Psychologist, 22*(1), 6–78.

Sexton, T. L., Whiston, S. C., Bleuer, J. C., & Walz, G. R. (1995). *A critical review of the counseling outcomes research.* Technical Report submitted to the Human Development Foundation, American Counseling Association.

Shapiro, D. A., Barkham, M., Hardy, G. E., & Morrison, L. A. (1990). The second Sheffield psychotherapy project: Rationale, design and preliminary outcome data. *British Journal of Medical Psychology, 63*(2), 97–108.

Shapiro, D. A., Barkham, M., Hardy, G. E., Reynolds, S., Rees, A., & Startup, M. (1994). Effects of treatment duration and severity of depression on the effectiveness of cognitive/behavioral and psychodynamic/interpersonal psychotherapy. *Journal of Consulting and Clinical Psychology, 62,* 522–534.

Shapiro, D. A., & Shapiro, D. (1982). Meta-analysis of comparative therapy outcome sudies: A reply to Wilson. *Behavioural Psychotherapy, 10*(4), 307–310.

Shaw, B. F. (1983, July). *Training therapists for the treatment of depression: Collaborative study.* Paper presented at the annual meeting of the Society for Psychotherapy Research, Sheffield, England.

Shaw, B. F., & Dobson, K. S. (1988). Competency judgments in the training and evaluation of psychotherapists. *Journal of Consulting and Clinical Psychology, 56,* 666–672.

Shoran-Salmon, V., & Rosenthal, R. (1989). Paradoxical interventions: A meta-analysis. *Journal of Consulting and Clinical Psychology, 55,* 22–28.

Singer, J. L. (1980). The scientific basis of psychotherapeutic practice: A question of values and ethics. *Psychotherapy: Theory, Research and Practice, 17,* 372–382.

Sledge, W. H., Moras, K., Hartley, D., & Levine, M. (1990). Effect of time-limited psychotherapy on patient dropout rates. *American Journal of Psychiatry, 147,* 1341–1347.

Sloan, R. B., Staples, F. R., Cristol, A. H., Yorkson, N. J., & Whipple, K. (1975). *Psychotherapy versus behavior therapy.* Cambridge, MA: Harvard University Press.

Smith, M. L., & Glass, G. V. (1977). Meta-analysis of psychotherapy outcome studies. *American Psychologist, 32*(9), 752–760.

Smith, M. L., Glass, G. V., & Miller, T. I. (1980). *The benefits of psychotherapy.* Baltimore: Johns Hopkins University Press.

Smith, S. E. (1994). Parent-initiated contracts: An intervention for school-related behaviors. *Elementary School Guidance and Counseling, 28,* 182–187.

Sokol, L., Beck, A. T., Greenberg, R. L., Wright, F. D., & Berchick, R. J. (1989). Cognitive therapy of panic disorder: A nonpharmacological alternative. *Journal of Nervous and Mental Disease, 12,* 711–716.

Speer, D. C. (1994). Can treatment research inform decision makers? Non-experimental method issues and examples among older outpatients. *Journal of Consulting and Clinical Psychology, 62,* 560–568.

Spokane, A. R. (1991). *Career interventions.* Englewood Cliffs, NJ: Prentice Hall.

Spokane, A. R., & Oliver, L. W. (1983). Research integration: Approaches, problems and recommendations for research reporting. *Journal of Counseling Psychology, 30,* 252–257.

Sprinthall, N. A. (1981). A new model for reseach in the service of guidance and counseling. *Personnel and Guidance Journal, 59*(8), 487–493.

St. Clair, K. L. (1989). Middle school counseling research: A resource for school counselors. *Elementary School Guidance and Counseling, 23,* 219–226.

Steenbarger, B. N. (1994). Duration and outcome in psychotherapy: An integrative review. *Professional Psychology: Research and Practice, 25,* 111–119.

Stein, D. M., & Lambert, M. J. (1995). Graduate training in psychotherapy: Are therapy outcomes enhanced? *Journal of Consulting and Clinical Psychology, 63,* 182–196.

Steinmetz, J. L., Lewinsohn, P. M., & Antonuccio, D. O. (1983). Prediction of individual outcome in a group intervention for depression. *Journal of Consulting and Clinical Psychology, 51,* 331–337.

Stiles, W. B., Shapiro, D. A., & Elliott, R. (1986). "Are all psychotherapies equivalent?" [Special issue: Psychotherapy research]. *American Psychologist, 41*(2), 165–180.

Stone, W. N., Green, B. L., Gleser, G. C., Whitman, R. M., & Roster, B. B. (1975). Impact of psychosocial factors on the conduct of combined drug and psychotherapy research. *British Journal of Psychiatry, 127,* 432–439.

Stricker, G. (1992). The relationship of research to clinical practice. *American Psychologist, 47,* 543–549.

Stricker, G., & Trierweiler, S. J. (1995). The local scientist: A bridge between science and practice. *American Psychologist, 50,* 995–1002.

Strong, S. R. (1968). Counseling: An interpersonal influence process. *Journal of Counseling Psychology, 15,* 215–224.

Strupp, H. H. (1989). Psychotherapy: Can the practitioner learn from the researcher? *American Psychologist, 47,* 543–549.

Stuhr, U., & Meyer, A. E. (1991). Hamburg Short Psychotherapy Comparison Experiment. In M. Crago & L. Beutler (Eds.), *Psychotherapy research: An international review of programmatic studies.* (pp. 212–218) Washington, DC: American Psychological Association.

Sue, S., Fujino, D. C., Hu, L., Takeuchi, D. T., & Zane, N. W. S. (1991). Community mental health services for ethnic minority groups: A test of the cultural responsiveness hypothesis. *Journal of Consulting and Clinical Psychology, 59,* 533–540.

Sue, S., McKinney, H., Allen, D., & Hall, J. (1974). Delivery of community mental health services to Black and White clients. *Journal of Consulting and Clinical Psychology, 42,* 794–801.

Suit, J. L., & Paradise, L. V. (1985). Effects of metaphors and cognitive complexity on perceived counselor characteristics. *Journal of Counseling Psychology, 32,* 23–28.

Super, D. E. (1957). *The psychology of careers.* New York: Harper.

Svartberg, M., & Stiles, T. C. (1991). Comparative effects of short-term psychodynamic psychotherapy: A meta-analysis. *Journal of Consulting and Clinical Psychology, 59*(5), 704–714.

Swanson, J. L. (1995). The process and outcome of career counseling. In W. B. Walsh & S. H. Osipow (Eds.), *Handbook of vocational psychology: Theory, research, and practice* (pp. 217–259). Mahwah, NJ: Erlbaum.

Target, M., & Fonagy, P. (1994). The efficacy of psychoanalysis for children: Prediction of outcome in a developmental context. *Journal of American Academy of Child and Adolescent Psychiatry, 33,* 1134–1144.

Terrell, R., & Terrell, S. (1984). Race of counselor, client sex, cultural mistrust level, and premature termination from counseling among Black clients. *Journal of Counseling Psychology, 31,* 371–375.

Teusch, L. (1990). Positive effects and limitations of client-centered therapy with schizophrenic patients. In G. Lietaer, J. Rombauts, & R. Van Balen (Eds.), *Client-centered and experiential psychotherapy in the nineties* (pp. 637–644). Leuven, Belgium: Leuven University Press.

Teusch, L., & Boehme, H. (1991). Results of a one-year follow-up of patients with agoraphobia and/or panic disorder treated with an inpatient therapy program with client-centered basis. *Psychotherapie-Psychosomatik Medizinische Psychologie, 41,* 68–76.

Thase, M. E., Bowler, K., & Harden, T. (1991). Cognitive behavior therapy of endogenous depression: II. Preliminary findings in 16 unmedicated inpatients. *Behavior Therapy, 22*(4), 469–477.

Thompson, L. W., & Gallagher, D. (1984). Efficacy of psychotherapy in the treatment of late-life depression [Special issue: Psychological treatment of unipolar depression]. *Advances in Behaviour Research and Therapy, 6*(2), 127–139.

Thompson, L. W., Gallagher, D., & Breckenridge, J. S. (1987). Comparative effectiveness of psychotherapies for depressed elders. *Journal of Consulting and Clinical Psychology, 55*(3), 385–390.

Thurer, S., & Hursh, N. (1981). Characteristics of the therapeutic relationship. In C. E Walker (Ed.), *Clinical practice of psychology* (pp. 62–82). Elmsford, NY: Pergamon.

Tichenor, V., & Hill, C. E. (1989). A comparison of six measures of working alliance. *Psychotherapy, 26,* 195–199.

Tollinton, H. J. (1973). Initial expectations and outcome. *British Journal of Medical Psychology, 46,* 251–257.

Tracey, T. J. (1977). Impact of intake procedures upon client attrition in a community mental health center. *Journal of Consulting and Clinical Psychology, 45,* 192–195.

Tracey, T. J. (1985). Dominance and outcome: A sequential examination. *Journal of Counseling Psychology, 32,* 119–122.

Tracey, T. J. (1986). The stages of influence in counseling and psychotherapy. In F. Dorn (Ed.), *The social influence process in counseling and psychotherapy* (pp. 107–116). Springfield, IL: Charles C Thomas.

Tracey, T. J. (1987). Stage differences in the dependencies of topic initiation and topic following behavior. *Journal of Counseling Psychology, 34,* 123–131.

Tracey, T. J. (1988). Relationship of responsibility attribution congruence to psychotherapy outcome. *Journal of Social and Clinical Psychology, 7*(2-3), 131–146.

Tracey, T. J. (1989). Client and therapist session satisfaction over the course of psychotherapy. *Psychotherapy, 26*(2), 177–182.

Tracey, T. J. (1993). An interpersonal stage model of the therapeutic process. *Journal of Counseling Psychology, 40*(4), 396–409.

Tracey, T. J. (1991). Counseling research as an applied science. In C. E. Watkins & L. J. Schneider (Eds.), *Research in counseling* (pp. 3–31). Hillsdale, NJ: Erlbaum.

Tracey, T. J., & Hayes, K. (1989). Therapist complementarity as a function of experience and client stimuli. *Psychotherapy, 26*(4), 462–468.

Truax, C. B., Wargo, D. G., & Silber, L. D. (1966). Effects of group psychotherapy with high accurate empathy and nonpossessive warmth upon female institutionalized delinquents. *Journal of Abnormal Psychology, 71,* 267–274.

Utay, J. M., & Lampe, R. E. (1995). Use of a group counseling game to enhance social skills of children with learning disabilities. *Journal for Specialists in Group Work, 20,* 114–120.

VandeCreek, L., & Angstadet, L. (1985). Client preferences and anticipations about counselor self-disclosure. *Journal of Counseling Psychology, 32,* 206–214.

Vandracek, F. W., Learner, R. M., & Schulenberg, S. E. (1986). *Career development: A life-span developmental approach.* Hillsdale, NJ: Erlbaum.

Verduyn, C. M., Lord, W., & Forrest, G. C. (1990). Social skills training in schools: An evaluation study. *Journal of Adolescence, 13*(1), 3–16.

Visser, S., Hoekstra, R. J., & Emmelkamp, P. M. G. (1992). Follow-up study on behavioural treatment of obsessive-compulsive disorders. In A. Ehlers, W. Fiegenbaum, I. Florin, & J. Margraf (Eds.), *Perspectives and promises of clinical psychology* (pp. 157–170). New York: Plenum.

Walz, G. R., Bleuer, J. C., & Bohall, R. A. (1996). *Treasure Chest II.* Greensboro: ERIC Counseling and Student Services Clearinghouse, University of North Carolina at Greensboro.

Watkins, C. E. (1990). The effects of counselor self-disclosure: A research review. *The Counseling Psychologist, 18*(3), 447–500.

Watkins, C. E., Savickas, M. L., Brizzi, J., & Manus, M. (1990). Effects of counselor response behavior on clients' impressions during vocational counseling. *Journal of Counseling Psychology, 37,* 138–142.

Watkins, C. E., & Schneider, L. J. (1989). Self-involving versus self-disclosing counselor statements during an initial interview. *Journal of Counseling and Development, 67,* 345–349.

Webster-Stratton, C., Hollinsworth, T., & Kolpacoff, M. (1989). The long-term effectiveness of treatment and clinical significance of three cost-effective training programs for families with conduct problem children. *Journal of Consulting and Clinical Psychology, 57,* 550–553.

Weighill, V. E., Hodge, J., & Peck, D. F. (1983). Keeping appointments with clinical psychologists. *The British Journal of Clinical Psychology, 22,* 143–144.

Weissberg, R. P., Caplan, M., & Harwood, R. L. (1991). Promoting competent young people in competence-enhancing environments: A systems-based perspective on primary prevention. *Journal of Consulting and Clinical Psychology, 59,* 830–841.

Weisz, J. R., Rudolph, K. D., Granger, D. A., & Sweeney, L. (1992). Cognition, competence and coping in child and adolescent depression: Research findings, developmental concerns, therapeutic implications. *Development and Psychopathology, 4,* 627–654.

Weisz, J. R., Weiss, V., Alicke, M. D., & Klotz, M. L. (1987). Effectiveness of psychotherapy with children and adolescents: A meta-analysis for clinicians. *Journal of Consulting and Clinical Psychology, 55*(4), 542–549.

Wells, E. A., Hawkins, J. D., & Catalano, R. F. (1988). Choosing drug use measures for treatment outcome studies. 1. The influence of measurement approach on treatment results. *International Journal of Addictions, 23,* 851–873.

Whiston, S. C. (1996) Accountability through action research: Research methods for practitioners. *Journal of Counseling and Development,74,* 616–623.

Whiston, S. C., & Sexton, T. L. (1993). An overview of psychotherapy outcome research: Implications for practice. *Professional Psychology: Research and Practice, 24*(1), 43–51.

Whiston, S. C., & Sexton, T. L. (1995, April). *Increasing career counseling effectiveness: What research tells us.* Paper presented at the annual meeting of the American Counseling Association, Denver, CO.

Whiston, S. C., & Sexton, T. L. (1996). *Outcome research and the components of comprehensive developmental guidance programs.* Manuscript submitted for publication.

Whiston, S. C., Sexton, T. L., & Lasoff, D. L. (1996). *Career intervention outcome: An extension of Oliver and Spokane.* Unpublished manuscript.

White, J., Keenam, M., & Brooks, N. (1992). Stress control: A controlled comparative investigation of large group therapy for generalized anxiety disorder. *Behavioural Psychotherapy, 20*(2), 97–113.

Wiggins, J. D., & Moody, A. H. (1987). Student evaluations of counseling programs: An added dimension. *School Counselor, 34*(5), 353–361.

Wiggins, J. D., & Wiggins, M. M. (1992). Elementary students' self-esteem and behavioral ratings related to counselor time-task emphases. *The School Counselor, 39,* 377–381.

Wiggins, J. G. (1992, May). Practice guidelines: Fundamentally wrong. *APA Monitor,* p. 3.

Williams, S. L. (1985). On the nature and measurement of agoraphobia. *Progress in Behavior Modification, 19,* 109–144.

Willis, R. M., Faither, S. L., & Snyder, D. K. (1987). Distinctiveness of behavioral versus insight-oriented marital therapy: An empirical analysis. *Journal of Consulting and Clinical Psychology, 55*(5), 685–690.

Wilson, N. S. (1985). School counselors and research: Obstacles and opportunities. *The School Counselor, 33,* 111–119.

Wilson, N. S. (1986). Effects of a classroom guidance unit on sixth graders' examination performance. *Journal of Humanistic Education and Development, 25*(2), 70–79.

Wirt, W. M. (1967). Psychotherapeutic persistence. *Journal of Consulting Psychology, 31,* 429.

Wynne, M. E., Susman, M., Ries, S., Birringer, J., & Katz, L. (1994). A method for assessing therapist's recall of in-session events. *Journal of Counseling Psychology, 41,* 53–57.

Yankelovitz, D. (April, 1990). *Public attitudes toward people with chronic mental illness.* Wahington, DC: Robert Wood Johnson Program in Mental Illness.

Yeaton, W., & Sechreist, L. (1981). Critical dimensions in the choice and maintenance of successful treatments: Strength, integrity, and effectiveness. *Journal of Consulting and Clinical Psychology, 67,* 156–167.

Zill, N., & Schoenborn, C. A. (1990). Developmental, learning, and emotional problems: Health of our nation's children, United States, 1988. *National Center for Health Statistics.* Hyattsville, MD: U.S. Department of Health and Human Services.

Index